William Doyle is Emeritus Professor of History at the University of Bristol, and Fellow of the British Academy. Among his many publications are *The Oxford History of the French Revolution* (2nd edn., 2002) and an earlier volume of essays, *Officers, Nobles, and Revolutionaries* (1995). More recent books include *Aristocracy and its Enemies in the Age of Revolution* (2009) and the edited *Oxford Handbook of the Ancien Régime* (2011).

This book reveals the ever fertile mind of Bill Doyle in all its many facets, from the carefully researched, intricate minutiae of venality and finance in ancien régime France, to the grand sweep of the fall of monarchies and the roots of revolution across the Western world in the Age of Revolutions. There is a fresh insight and a refreshing dash of much needed iconoclasm, on every page. Doyle is a scholar who continues to provoke, instruct and inspire, in prose as sparkling and clear as a vintage Champagne.'

Michael Broers, Professor of Western European History, University of Oxford

'Here is William Doyle at his finest. In this book, distilling his most recent research, this master historian of the Old Regime and French Revolution explores key issues in the collapse, and rebuilding of French state and society from Louis XIV through Napoleon. In typical Doyle fashion, the chapters emphasize contingency, complexity and continuity. By steering clear of determinisms and refusing to treat the French Revolution as inevitable, Doyle makes palpable the sense of possibility that infused those heady times.'

Rafe Blaufarb, Professor of History and Director of the Institute on Napoleon and the French Revolution, Florida State University

'In recent decades William Doyle has been the leading British historian of France's evolution from ancien régime to Revolution and beyond. This welcome collection of incisive short studies throws illuminating and, at times, unexpected light on this trajectory and will be essential for all who study or teach Europe's long-eighteenth century.'

Professor Hamish Scott, University of Glasgow

FRANCE *and the age of* REVOLUTION

Regimes Old and New from Louis XIV to Napoleon Bonaparte

WILLIAM DOYLE

I.B. TAURIS

LONDON · NEW YORK

Published in 2013 by I.B.Tauris & Co. Ltd
6 Salem Road, London W2 4BU
175 Fifth Avenue, New York NY 10010
www.ibtauris.com

Distributed in the United States and Canada Exclusively by Palgrave Macmillan
175 Fifth Avenue, New York NY 10010

International Library of Historical Studies: 91

ISBN: 978 1 78076 444 3 (HB)
978 1 78076 445 0 (PB)

A full CIP record for this book is available from the British Library
A full CIP record is available from the Library of Congress

Library of Congress Catalog Card Number: available

Typeset by Newgen Publishers, Chennai
Printed and bound in Great Britain by T.J. International, Padstow, Cornwall

MIX
Paper from
responsible sources
FSC
www.fsc.org
FSC® C013056

Contents

Part III: Napoleon: An Undemocratic Revolutionary

Illustrations

Introduction

Sell one's influence, bribery

Most of the essays in this collection have appeared since the publication of *Venality: The Sale of Offices in Eighteenth-Century France* in 1996. In that book I attempted to analyse the structure, operation, and implications of a practice which lay at the heart of how institutions and elite social life worked in pre-revolutionary France. The abolition of venality was one of the most radical and enduring of all the reforms of the French Revolution. Its ramifications were so far-reaching that no single volume could do complete justice to them.

Part I of the present book explores some aspects of venality that a general survey could only have discussed in unbalancing detail. The only piece falling outside the Age of Revolution concerns the attempts of Louis XIV's great minister Colbert to rein in its growth, and his hopes of getting rid of it altogether. His failure illustrates the scale and intractability of the problem, and, by implication, why it took a revolution to bring his dreams to fruition. Colbert himself owed much of his rise to the opportunities offered his family by venality; and throughout its history few even of its fiercest critics were completely untainted by it. Among the most celebrated after Colbert was Voltaire, whose hostility turns out to have been far more equivocal than has often been assumed, and directed overwhelmingly against a magistracy which attracted his contempt largely for quite different reasons. The venal instinct penetrated into some most unlikely places, including the church. Although simony, the sale of priestly functions, was one of the oldest and most execrated of abuses, in France other positions confined to priests were open to purchase. Yet few clergy defended venality, any more than most of the laymen who wrote about it. There was, in fact, a massive consensus against it, regarding it as a virulent form of corruption. The problem remained not simply how to eliminate it, but how to do without it. Some critics feared that, however undesirable, some sort of corruption was a necessary evil in public life. Nor was this perception confined to France. Across the Channel in Great Britain and in Ireland there was relatively little venality outside the army, but corruption seemed just as pervasive in other ways, and perhaps just as necessary. Yet over the Age of Revolution, roughly between 1770 and 1850, corruption of the old sort was largely eliminated in both France and Great Britain. It was a great turning point in the history of political culture, and a final essay in this section explores the very different routes by which two polities arrived at the same destination in abandoning the instinctive ways of their old regimes.

Even in Great Britain one of the major forces bringing this about was the French Revolution. Having spent many years, thanks to an unlikely chapter of accidents, teaching the history of Ireland in the revolutionary age, an invitation to discuss the Irish Union of 1801 in a European context gave me the opportunity to contribute to debates on how far Great Britain in the eighteenth century might be called an ancien régime. Nevertheless most of Part II reflects on how the French destroyed theirs. The main theme of the various essays is to emphasise the role of choice and contingency. In the mid-twentieth century, writing about the French Revolution was pervaded by a certain economic and social determinism, much of it inspired by Marxism. Between the 1950s and the 1980s the empirical underpinning of this approach was chipped away by what became known as revisionism. But many, especially in France and across the Atlantic, worried that revisionism had exorcised Marxism while 'putting nothing in its place'. Why something was needed in its place was far from obvious; but those who felt the need eagerly embraced the so-called cultural or linguistic 'turns' sweeping through wider history writing by this time. The result was a post-revisionism in which cultural and linguistic determinism came to replace the old economic and social varieties. Two essays here take issue with some of the results. While post-revisionists tend to accept that the Revolution had to become 'thinkable' before it became possible, I argue quite the opposite. Some also believe that the regicide which was one of the crucial events of the Revolution could not have come about without a long-maturing pre-revolutionary 'desacralisation' of the French monarchy. It has seemed to me ever since the idea was first mooted that no such process can be demonstrated convincingly, and that it is not in fact necessary for explaining the overthrow of monarchy. Nobody dreamed of executing Louis XVI in 1789. It was the unprecedented, hitherto *un*thinkable events of the Revolution itself which largely explain his fate. The course of those events is revisited in a further set of reflections on how the Revolution transformed attitudes to monarchy and its basis in France and beyond. Fully a year before the French Revolution turned republican, the revolutionaries also attempted to abolish the social elite previously inseparable from royal government, the nobility. On that occasion, the lead was taken by nobles themselves, who, ever since their eager participation in the republican revolt across the Atlantic, had heedlessly embraced ideas and developments deeply dangerous for the interests of their own order.

This is a theme I have explored at greater length in *Aristocracy and its Enemies in the Age of Revolution* (2009). There I followed the fortunes of nobility through abolition, emigration and Terror to show that although the revolutionaries denied it any recognition, they were unable to destroy nobility as they intended. Napoleon, in fact, revived it in a new form: and one of the essays in Part

III discusses some remaining problems concerning the imperial elite. Only in the most superficial sense can this creation be described as a betrayal of the Revolution; and the same can be said of Napoleon's notorious marginalisation of women, which seems much in line with what leading feminist historians have seen as the deep misogyny of the Jacobins. Napoleon has been a late interest for me, and only one of the four pieces in Part III has been published before. On the political culture of his empire, it explores how far he drew on instinctive French reflexes long predating the Revolution (in the original version, delivered as a conference paper, I suggested calling them memes, but the audience discouraged me from going on with this). In the end, however, I conclude that Napoleon did far more to consolidate the work of the Revolution than to reverse it. His reputation as the Revolution's gravedigger seems to be largely based upon an assumption that its essence lay in the Jacobin republic, much of whose Terror-haunted work he did indeed repudiate. But, apart from sullying the reputation of republicanism in Europe for three generations, Jacobinism achieved nothing enduring. The earlier years of the Revolution, by contrast, destroyed the ancien régime and rationalised French public life for ever. Napoleon welcomed both achievements as the bedrock of his new regime. He then used his power to extend them to Europe beyond France, with unavoidable ramifications in its extensive overseas dominions. These achievements too were never reversed. Bonapartist authoritarianism, it is true, had little content beyond nostalgia, and was to have no longer-term future than Jacobinism. Perhaps that was because its true destiny, the destruction of Europe's old order, had already been accomplished by its founder.

PART I

FUNCTIONS FOR SALE

Jean-Baptiste Colbert (1619–1683) by Antoine Coysevox

CHAPTER 1

Colbert and the Sale
of Offices

W hen in the later Middle Ages kings began to realise that they could no longer wage war effectively by raising feudal levies, they were compelled to look for unprecedented sums instead to fund professional warriors. They realised at the same time that they would never be able to find the necessary sums through taxation alone. Soon seeing themselves as overtaxed, their subjects resisted their demands either by evasion or simply by refusing to pay; and states lacked the means of assessment and compulsion to back up their demands, especially among their richest subjects who found means to avoid at least the majority of direct taxes. Great orders or corporate bodies, such as the church or the nobility, soon proved able to formulate excellent reasons for exemption that no king was able to set aside. Above all, the liquid wealth of mercantile groups completely escaped fiscal demands.

These were the problems that gave rise to the sale of offices. By selling public offices, in other words farming out portions of the royal authority to persons prepared to pay for it, kings found a way of persuading holders of liquid capital to place it in their hands. Nor was it only their own capital. Office-holders themselves could borrow more on the security of their offices; and by varying the powers and privileges attached to them, a king could find further occasions to make their holders borrow and pay out.

And so in the sixteenth century the sale and manipulation of offices became widespread in European monarchies. It was found in the Spanish Empire and the states of the Pope, in England, and in several German principalities.[1] But nowhere was venality more widespread or more systematically exploited than in France. It was already well established when, in the 1520s, King Francis I set up the Office of Parts Casual (*bureau des parties casuelles*) to serve, in the famous words of the jurist Loyseau, 'as a stall for selling this new merchandise'.

Given that, ever since 1467, an office was defined as a function of which no holder could be deprived except by death, resignation, or forfeiture, it was the soundest of investments. Very soon, most of the king's offices were venalised, and their number never ceased to multiply. Entire new categories of offices were created simply for selling, without the slightest regard for sound administration. Between 1515 and 1610, their number rose from around 4–5,000 to about 25,000, most of them judicial offices. The advantages attached to venal offices reached their peak in 1604 with the introduction of the Paulette or annual due (its official name, usually shortened to *annuel*) which guaranteed the free transmission of an office to a named successor, heir, or buyer in return for the payment of a fee worth one sixth of its official valuation (*finance*). This protected the officer from the operation of the so-called forty-day rule (introduced in the 1530s) under which, if an officer happened to die within 40 days of relinquishing an office, it reverted to the king or, as the phrase went, 'fell to the Parts Casual'. The only worry office-holders might still have was over the renewal of the *annuel*, which was normally only granted for a period of nine years. The king might always choose not to renew it, which would upset the matrimonial strategies of thousands of families whose property and fortunes were bound up in offices.

Almost inevitably, therefore, any renewal by the king offered him the chance to demand extra payments from officers in order to retain the privileges of 'admission' to the payment of the *annuel*.

French society and institutions in the seventeenth century were deeply marked by the development of venality. Office purchase became the main ladder of social mobility for the elites, and several thousand ennobling offices at the summit of the system opened nobility to the ambitions of the richest commoners. The body of office-holders made up a powerful network of interests, and each company fiercely protected its corner of the system. At the same time, the king came to depend more and more on venality. His 'casual' revenues, essentially what venality brought in, made up an important proportion of the royal finances. In the year when Richelieu entered the Thirty Years' War, casual revenues made up no less than 40 per cent of the king's income.[2] And, since the alienation of royal authority represented by the sale of an office was never more than temporary, capital advanced in this way could never be considered more than a loan. The king could not suppress an office without reimbursing the holder. And so, despite repeated promises by monarchs and regents throughout the sixteenth and seventeenth centuries to abolish venality, reimburse office-holders, and recruit servants of the state on merit, it was never seriously possible to think of such a policy because of its prohibitive cost. It is probable that the point of no return in this process had already been reached as early as the reign of Henry II (1547–1559), when the renewal of Italian wars brought renewed expansion of venality.[3] The creation under Henry IV of the *annuel* marked in turn a recognition of the fact that it was better to milk systematically a system which could not be got rid of. This approach reached its peak under Richelieu who, while deploring the principle of venality, realised the practical impossibility of doing without it, and exploited it to its very limits.

It was under the ministry of Richelieu that Jean-Baptiste Colbert entered the circles of power. He did so in 1640 when his father bought for him the office of commissioner for war (*commissaire des guerres*). He passed some time at the beginning of his career in the office of François Sabathier, Treasurer of the Parts Casual,[4] thus learning very early on how the venal system worked, not to mention the operations of the great state financiers and the dangers brought on by their bankruptcies (like that of Sabathier himself in 1641) for the stability of the crown's finances.[5] Later, as a clerk to Secretary of State Michel Le Tellier, and his link-man to Mazarin, he found himself at the centre of the state's affairs at the time of the crisis which led to the Fronde. Notoriously, the Fronde began with a revolt of office-holders. Triggered by new financial demands prior to the renewal of the *annuel* in April 1648, the Fronde quickly developed into a protest movement, led by the magistrates of the Parlement of Paris, against the suspension of interest payments (*gages*) attached to offices, against new office creations, against the extortionate demands of the *traitants* or *partisans* who managed the market in offices, and against the loss of jurisdiction by courts made up of venal officers in favour of non-venal commissioners in the form of the intendants. Colbert, by then a Counsellor of State and so close to the centre of power, was able to observe how this resistance imperilled the kingdom's war effort, and finally plunged it into civil war. The latter in turn almost destroyed the career of this man on the rise when, in 1651, Mazarin, the patron to whom he had sworn loyalty, was driven into exile. Colbert was reduced simply to managing the affairs of the absent cardinal. These experiences seem to have determined his attitude towards officers in general, and the whole system of venality.

Although the defeat of the Fronde and the uncontested return of Mazarin to power brought a renewal of many of the 'innovations' condemned by the magistrates of the parlementary Fronde (*gages* in arrear, return of intendants, renewed reliance on *traitants* and *partisans*) Mazarin did not stubbornly carry on as if nothing had happened. It was true that the war, which as before continued to drive the exploitation of venality, continued until 1659, but the creation of new offices slowed markedly and when the *annuel* was renewed in 1657 there were no new conditions or financial demands. In this Mazarin followed the advice of Fouquet, who as procurator-general of the parlement thought himself best placed to manage it, and as Superintendant of the Finances sought to persuade the court not to impede new financial edicts necessary for the final resolution of the Spanish war.[6]

But already Colbert did not like Fouquet's approach. He thought there was nothing to be gained by protecting the interests of office-holders, at whatever level.[7] When in the autumn of 1659 Mazarin asked his opinion on the state of the finances, Colbert condemned the short-term expedients so far favoured by the Superintendant. And although, like the Frondeurs of 1648, he advised the setting up of a special Chamber of Justice to make *traitants* pay back their excessive and illicit profits, that was the only way in which his ideas matched those of the office-holders and chimed in with their interests. For Colbert, the essential corollary of diminishing the power of *traitants* was to reduce at the same time the privilege of office-holders, whose exploitation offered the financiers so many of their so-called 'extraordinary affairs'. He advised starting by cutting the *gages* and fiscal privileges of ten thousand officers in the Bureaux of Finances, and minor financial jurisdictions like the *élections* and the salt stores (*greniers à sel*). Then the number of offices themselves could be cut.

> To this end [he wrote] we might take away their annual due, diminish their *gages* and rights, and order the price of one or two offices of every sort on a footing of the last one sold, in each generality

or election, always beginning by reimbursing the youngest; by so doing, with justice to all, we might bring down all these offices over the time of 3 or 4 years to the tenth part of the number of officers living on what they draw from the people, raising the number of those subject to the taille who would be the richest and would give the people more means of paying their taxes. The king would also derive an infinitely more considerable advantage than that, which is that more than 20000 men who lived throughout the kingdom by means of these great abuses which have slipped into the finances, will be obliged to apply themselves to trade and to manufactures, to agriculture and to war, which are the only occupations which render the kingdom flourishing.[8]

After that it would be possible to

work at the reduction of the multiplicity of officers of sovereign and subordinate jurisdictions, of the abuses committed in justice, and to have it dispensed to the people more promptly and at less cost, it being certain that officers of justice draw from the people of the realm every year, by an infinity of means, more than 20 millions of pounds which there would be much justice in diminishing by more than three quarters, which would render the people more comfortable and would leave them more means to provide for the expenses of the state; and further, there being more than 30000 men living from justice in the whole extent of the kingdom, if it were reduced to the point where it ought to be, 7 or 8000 at the most would be sufficient, and the rest would be obliged to employ themselves in commerce, in agriculture or in warfare, and they would work in consequence to the advantage and the good of the kingdom, instead of only working as at present to its destruction. Should his Eminence so desire, notes can be sent to him of all these increases in officers of justice which have been made for 50 or 60 years, and the means that could be employed to reduce them, without risk of any outcry...[9]

Mazarin took no notice of this suggestion; but the memorandum of Colbert clearly shows a first sketch of several ideas which would drive his policies once the cardinal had disappeared and Fouquet was eliminated, with the agreement of the young Louis XIV.

Louis XIV certainly had his own reasons for mistrusting office-holders. He had not forgotten, nor ever would, the humiliating treatment he had received at their hands during the Fronde. He blamed rebellious magistrates for launching this movement, 'parlements still in possession of and relishing usurped authority'.[10] At the same time he deplored 'offices filled by chance and by money, rather than by choice and by merit; the inexperience of some judges, lacking in knowledge; rules on age and length of service evaded almost everywhere'.[11] He concluded that 'reform was necessary. My affairs were not in a state such that I need fear anything from their discontent. Rather it was fitting to show them that there was nothing to fear from them, and that times had changed.'[12]

What change would mean could be seen immediately after the fall of Fouquet. One of the last acts of the Superintendant in August 1661 was an edict abolishing all *élections* established since 1630, and reducing the number of offices in those remaining. The Court of Aids of Paris resisted it, and finally the edict was transcribed on to the registers of the court in the presence of Monsieur, representing his brother the king. Everyone assumed, tacitly, that this was an abolition of a sort that had become normal since the 1630s, something which the king would be prepared to annul for an appropriate payment from those concerned. Accordingly, the *élus* offered 61 millions to be kept in being. But this offer only arrived at the beginning of 1662, several months after the fall of Fouquet, and now Colbert was in charge. The offer was refused, and the government proceeded to liquidate the offices as the edict prescribed.[13] Colbert had the same ambition for officers in the salt stores, condemned to abolition in the same edict, but he had to recognise that the cost of such a liquidation was too high for the moment. He confined himself to depriving them of the *annuel*, so that these offices were liable to fall into the Parts Casual if their holders happened to die within 40 days of relinquishing them,

> so that by this means [his Majesty] would free his people in three or four years of the vexations that a great number of officers of this sort make them suffer, would profit by their death from the *gages* and rights which belong to them, would not need to reimburse them, and even hold considerable funds in his Parts Casual in the fixed value (*taxe*) of these vacant offices, to make use of on a pressing occasion.[14]

This would become one of Colbert's key strategies for cutting down venality. As much as possible, hereditary or reversionary (*à survivance*) offices would be transformed into casual ones so as to increase the chances of seeing them fall to the crown or at least produce a regular revenue through the *annuel*. Thus, whereas in 1633 only half of all officers had paid it, by 1665 the proportion had risen to three quarters.[15] Meanwhile, Colbert sought by every means to save the king money. On arriving in power, by an *arrêt* of the council of October 1661, he ordered the reduction by a third of all augmentations of *gages* (on additional interest-bearing capital) granted since 1635.[16] There was general consternation, and the sovereign courts protested, but no notice was taken. Finally a Chamber of Justice was set up to review the conduct of *traitants* and financiers since 1635,[17] and meanwhile their opportunities of profiting from venality were diminished by abolishing three and four year job-sharing. Certain great financial posts even ceased to be venal and became revocable commissions, including that of General Treasurer of the Parts Casual itself. It all proved easier that had been thought. As Colbert explained to the king in October 1664, in a note echoing that sent to Mazarin five years previously:[18]

> The two professions which uselessly consume a hundred thousand of your subjects without contributing to your glory, are finance and justice.

Finance absorbs more than thirty thousand. You have already destroyed this monster, which was certainly most difficult and most terrible, because it absorbed all other conditions; Your Majesty has seen however how easily you have brought it about.

Justice is particular in that besides absorbing 70 thousand men and more, it imposes a weighty and tyrannical yoke, under the authority of your name, on all the rest of your people: through chicanery, it keeps more than a million occupied.

And yet the diminution of these burdens on the king's subjects and on his finances would be a long drawn out process. A programme would need to be pursued over several years. And, as in all he undertook, Colbert preferred to act on precise information. This was why in May 1665 he ordered the Bureaux of Finances to send him a list of all offices of justice and finance in their jurisdictions, with current prices, *gages* received, official valuations, and the revenue produced by their *annuel*. The overall results, for the year 1664, can be summarised as follows:[19]

Number of offices	45,780
Current price	419,630,842
Gages	8,346,847
Valuation	187,276,978
Annuel	2,002,447

The list was still incomplete in a number of ways. It included neither members of the King's Household nor military posts. But certain results were clear. First the market value of offices was twice that of valuations, which had remained unchanged since 1638. Secondly, since the *annuel* was calculated on the 1638 valuations, it brought in far less for the king than he might legitimately hope. Finally, the king was spending four times more in *gages* than he was receiving from the *annuel*.

Other less direct conclusions were also possible, as the eighteenth-century historian of the finances Véron de Forbonnais, a great admirer of Colbert, saw.[20] First, there were too many officers:

> We see from this Tabulation that there were forty-five thousand seven hundred and eighty Families to do work for which six thousand would have been enough. [Then,] four hundred and nineteen millions six hundred and forty two pounds were diverted from agriculture, from the arts and from Commerce. It was much more than two thirds of the mass of money existing in the state; & in supposing that half of this sum alone was taken from that sort of work, interest on the money should have been lower by a third.

It can scarcely be doubted that most of these thoughts resulted from Forbonnais's reading of the papers of Colbert, echoing the thinking of the minister himself. And for all these matters, an opportune moment was coming: the expiry of the *annuel* in 1666. How might the king take advantage? The most attractive expedient might be not to renew it.

> It is certain, [thought Colbert[21]] that no moment will be more favourable. The King is feared, loved and obeyed more than any king before him, without comparison; he is enjoying universal peace. He has no trouble to dread within the kingdom, and the advantages which the state will receive will be troubled by no apprehensions. The entire consideration and credit of the men of the robe will be entirely overturned by this step alone. Reform of justice will be accomplished much more easily…merchants will be much more respected in the kingdom, which will derive great advantages. The greater part of the kingdom's money employed in that trade, will flow back in time into commerce truly useful to the state.

At the same time there would be important economic advantages:[22]

The consideration, the credit of this venality, along with what the wiles of men adds in rights, *épices* [judicial fees] and other indirect advantages, have pushed up their prices prodigiously, such that perhaps all the lands in the kingdom estimated according to their true value could not pay the price of all the offices of judicature and finance.

These same reasons mean that any man, son of a merchant or another, with any means has always borrowed the rest of what he needed to make himself an officer of a sovereign court, hoping that through a marriage or through some other advantage he might make it up: and this madness has reached such a point that it can be held certain that half at least of these holders of offices are in debt for part of them, such that not only the fortune of all officers, who are at least 20000 in the kingdom, consists in what they persuade themselves their office is worth, but even that of the same number of their creditors.

In the event, by an edict of December 1665 the *annuel* was renewed. Perhaps the danger of war following the death of Philip IV of Spain in September aroused fears that this source of revenue could not be forgone. On the other hand, it was not renewed for the usual nine years, but only for three. This unprecedented abridgement seemed to indicate that the intention was to abandon the *annuel* entirely as soon as possible. This would open the way, as with the officers of the salt stores deprived of it in 1661, to a gradual diminution of the number of officers as these fell into the Parts Casual as a result of the 40-day rule.

Yet all this still left shrinking the number of offices dependent on chance alone, which hardly squared with Colbert's 'more systematic than methodical mind'.[23] To keep control of bringing down the number of offices in the king's interest, the government had to be in a position to abolish them at a moment of its own choosing. This in turn raised the question of reimbursing their value – that fundamental obstacle to total abolition. The natural interest of the king was to pay off offices at the lowest possible price but, thanks to the confidence engendered by the *annuel,* the price of most offices had shot up since 1604.[24] Even the modified valuations of 1638, as the enquiry of 1665 had demonstrated, remained far lower than market prices achieved in the 1660s. Colbert therefore decided to introduce a policy of price-control. It was incorporated in the edict which prolonged the *annuel* for three years. There was no question of keeping to the valuations of 1638. Admittedly this would have been beneficial for the king, but ruinous for anybody who had bought an office after that date, and would have produced profound discontent at an obvious financial injustice. Colbert had no intention of provoking another Fronde. So new valuations were established, lower it is true than current market prices, but much higher than those of 1638. In the Parlement of Paris, for example, presidencies changing hands at 500,000 *livres* were fixed at 350,000, offices of counsellor selling at 123,000 *livres* were valued at 100,000.[25] Office-holders were forbidden to sell beyond these prices, and the king declared that, in the event of abolition, he would not reimburse those losing them at a higher price, even if they had paid out more.

This state of affairs would last until 1709. Although very unpopular to start with, needing a *lit de justice* in the presence of the king himself to get it registered, with the manifest intention of humiliating the magistrates through a show of royal authority,[26] it proved possible to circumvent the law for several years by the expedient of unofficial supplementary payments, the notorious *pots de vin.* Until these were prohibited in the 1670s,[27] they prevented sales at a loss, and from time to time might yield a profit. It is worth noting on the other hand that high prices did not always suit magistrates, at least in the Parlement of Paris: prices which ran beyond the means of the 'senatorial' class seemingly opened the way to candidates with little preparation for judicial life, such as the sons of *traitants* or financiers, from families without robe traditions. In reality, the number of candidates of this type had always been more modest than magistrates liked to think; but once *pots de vin* were forbidden, fixed prices became a reality, and, to the general satisfaction of the court, the number of candidates of low background fell.[28] Such considerations scarcely troubled the magistrates of the Parlement of Brittany, who had long been recruited from a fairly high social level; but the Rennes magistrates held out against fixed prices in their court for two whole years.[29] Later, the price of their offices fell far below the level fixed by Colbert, but this was perhaps mainly owing to their 24-year exile in Vannes as a result of their role in the Stamped Paper revolt of 1675.

Clearing the way for abolitions was not the only goal of Colbert in fixing the price of offices. To limit their constant rise would have the effect at the same time of limiting the capital required to buy them. The official rate of interest paid by the government was reduced on the very day the edict of 1665 appeared – surely no coincidence.[30] There is no doubt that Colbert and his master were delighted to humiliate the parlements; but nothing suggests that their policy on offices formed part of a deeper plan to eliminate these courts in the governance of the kingdom. Nor does anything suggest that they were thinking of abolishing tenure, that fundamental principle of the law of 1467. Colbert's ambition was above all economic: to stop the diversion of capital and human energy into offices, privileges, and the idleness which went with them, at the expense of more productive investments in trade and industry. These were long-term ambitions; and although Colbert believed that the first steps could be achieved quite quickly and that 'great strokes are accomplished as quickly in France as small, and that straight afterwards they are thought no more of'[31] at the same time he knew perfectly well that unforeseen crises could block great ambitions at any moment. 'It is certain enough', he wrote in 1665, 'that great strokes ought not to be put off, for fear of the ordinary accidents of a great state, which often take away the means to execute them. And, once put off, it can be held as certain that wars and other great accidents will prevent their execution.'

This is exactly what happened. Just as the death of Philip IV had prevented the entire abolition of the *annuel*, fresh rumours of wars prevented its abolition after three years. From the middle of 1669 it was becoming obvious, even to Colbert, that the king was planning before long to make war either on the Spaniards or the Dutch, or even on both at once.[32] In these circumstances it would have been very unwise to give up any financial resource. And so the *annuel*, far from being suppressed as the minister had hoped, was quietly prolonged for the usual nine years. Politically, Colbert continued to glory in the abolition of useless offices. In December 1670 he boasted that 20,000 had been got rid of since the king's accession.[33] The process went on until 1671, when 861 offices in the salt stores were bought out, and the number of treasurers of France in each Bureau of Finances was reduced to 12. These operations saved the king 5,260,032 *livres*.[34] But it is noteworthy that during this same year the creation of new offices resumed. The *annuel* was now offered to office-holders who had not enjoyed it before, such as the treasurers of France. Then in the year 1671 came the abandonment of another principle that Colbert had pursued since 1661, the transformation of as many offices as possible into casual ones. Once again, for a fee, reversionary tenure was offered to the king's secretaries and officers in the marshalcy, while heredity was sold to notaries, procurators and ushers.[35] The overall revenue of the Parts Casual, which had fallen to the lowest level of the reign in 1669 (458,936 *livres*) rose the next year by around 700 per cent (to 3,198,183 *livres*), to fall back in 1671 to 1,945,169.[36] No doubt this latter fall is evidence of Colbert's last attempts to hold the line. But after the famous 'Octave de Monsieur Colbert' of November 1671, when the king ordered him to find the money to pay for his military preparations or to make way for somebody else prepared to do it,[37] casual revenues shot up until 1674. Preparations for war, and its subsequent launch, destroyed any hope of continuing reform; and Colbert resigned himself to exploiting venality with as little scruple as any of his predecessors to sustain the ambitions of his master. As Forbonnais observed, 'the history of the finances henceforth offers us nothing but extraordinary affairs, not all of which turned out well'.[38]

Besieged by *traitants* to whom his door had remained closed for a decade, the minister soon found himself authorising a proliferation of brand new offices.[39] New offices were added to the chambers of accounts. In February 1674 a second Châtelet, the Paris court of first instance, was created to share the jurisdiction of the original. The king made 2 millions from that. At a much lower level, the craft of wigmaking, which had boomed since the arrival of the fashion for wigs during the 1660s, was venalised from top to bottom in 1673. Innumerable petty financial offices reappeared at the same time, such as veal vendors, sellers of sucking pigs, poultry, fish, or leather; measurers and brokers for all sorts of spirits; grain measurers; wood carvers, corn chandlers. Office-holders were also sold privileges such as exemption from the *taille*,[40] or heredity. In 1673 the king declared that he would bestow (that is to say, sell) age-dispensations on candidates for the magistracy who had not reached the age specified by law. It marked the abandonment of a campaign going back to 1662 to prevent younger people taking office.[41] Finally, when the *annuel* reached its normal term in 1674, there was no problem about renewing it for a further nine years – as it happened, for the rest of Colbert's life. And the terms of renewal echoed those of times before the Fronde. Only officers accepting augmentations of *gages* were admitted.[42] Yet few among them were prepared to hold out against this new forced loan that the king was forcing upon them, and he made 2,800,000 *livres* from it.[43] Over the whole period of the Dutch War, Colbert raised more than 150 millions in extraordinary affairs, of which 60 millions came from the manipulation of offices and venality.[44]

And so, under pressure from a war which his royal master was determined to undertake, and which lasted far longer than planned, Colbert quite simply abandoned the policy on offices that he had pursued during his first decade in power. He realised that no king of France could undertake a large-scale war without recourse to a series of now-classic financial expedients. Had this experience converted him, like his hero Richelieu,[45] to seeing some use in venality? Not at all. Towards 1680, the war now over, he is found advising the king to 'diminish the number of offices just as soon as may be possible, because they are a burden on the finances, on the people and on the State. Reduce them gradually, by abolition or by buying out, to the number they stood at in 1600. The benefit and the advantage which would accrue to the people and to the State would be difficult to express.'[46]

As in 1661, he suggested making a start with the officers of petty jurisdictions, such as the *élections* and the salt stores. But by now neither the influence nor the energy of the once all-powerful minister with the king were what they had been, and he was never able to resume his former policies. Ironically, it was only under his successor that several expedients adopted during the Dutch War were revoked – such as the restoration of a single unified Châtelet in 1684.

We should not underestimate the scale of Colbert's ambitions. He was the only minister between Michel de l'Hôpital and the Revolution who thought it possible entirely to eliminate the sale of offices.[47] He even began the process with a certain determination. If it was really true that before 1670 he had abolished and reimbursed 20,000 offices (which only further research could confirm), it was the greatest single cut-back that venality was to experience before 1790.[48] Meanwhile, Colbert succeeded in halting the rise in the price of the most important offices for the first time since 1604.

A general rise in their price would not occur again until after the middle of the eighteenth century. And for more than a decade, the minister managed the king's finances practically without needing *traitants* and their *avis* (proposals) or *affaires extraordinaires*, while what he paid out in *gages* fell along with the number of officers.

Colbert's belief in the benefits of this policy never wavered. If he had enjoyed a prolonged period of peace he might well have made permanent progress. But as a minister his power depended entirely on the confidence and support of Louis XIV, a young and ambitious monarch who took pride in making war. Venality, of course, from the very beginning was the child of war: it was war which had provided its greatest boosts, whether under Francis I, under Henry II, under Charles IX, under Louis XIII. In time of war, the resources and the credit of companies of officers were an important source of revenue for kings who could never have paid for their operations from tax-revenue alone. For France, offices were the equivalent of the Bank of Amsterdam in the Dutch Republic or (from the 1690s) the Bank of England across the Channel, or, as Pierre Chaunu suggested, the mines of America for the king of Spain.[49] Only in the eighteenth century, after pushing the resources of office-holders to the very limit to help pay for the last two wars of Louis XIV, did loans raised on the international money market overtake venality as a source of credit. In other words: no venality, no war; no war, no venality.

Colbert understood this. He knew that war, whether against the Spaniards or the Dutch, would blight all his plans; but he refused to risk his ministerial position by confronting those calling for war at a moment when, as he well knew, they were telling the king what he wanted to hear.[50] So did he recognise that his policy on offices was sure to be defeated in the end? Or should we conclude, with Daniel Dessert,[51] that 'the total or partial defeat of many of his enterprises underlines the limits of a minister who had not understood the deeper wellsprings of the world he lived in'?

Voltaire by Jean-Antoine Houdon

CHAPTER 2

Voltaire and Venality: The Ambiguities of an Abuse

'In France,' wrote La Bruyère in 1688, 'much firmness and great breadth of mind are required to do without offices and employments, and thus be prepared to stay at home and do nothing.'[1] Yet the leisure of the sage, he reflected, taken up as it was in tranquil thought, conversation, and reading, was also a form of work. Writing certainly was, as the life of Voltaire bore witness. But his family background illustrated a corollary of La Bruyère's observation: it was difficult in France to find respectable employment that was not a *charge*. Voltaire's father (if indeed Arouet *père* was his father) was typical enough: he made his fortune as a Parisian notary. Having sold that office two years before the birth of his famous son, two years afterwards he bought the even more lucrative, more expensive, but less burdensome one of *receveur des épices à la chambre des comptes*.[2] Voltaire's maternal grandfather was *greffier criminel* at the parlement. When he was 15, his sister married a *correcteur de la chambre des comptes*, which was an ennobling office. Thus Voltaire grew up at the heart of the 'bourgeoisie parisienne d'offices',[3] in a family mid-way on the classic route from commerce (Arouet *grand-père* had been a draper) to nobility. It was an ambiance permeated with the values and rewards of venality.

So was that of the school to which he was sent. At Louis-le-Grand Voltaire rubbed shoulders with the sons of far more prestigious office-holders, most of them predestined to follow their fathers or other male relatives into public offices that were at the same time the private property of their families.[4] The years of Voltaire's schooling were also ones in which venality reached its widest extent in French history. Originating as a way for the king to borrow money from the ambitious, the sale of royal offices and the further exploitation of their buyers through a range of fiscal expedients had expanded enormously since the early sixteenth century.[5] By 1664 it was estimated that there were at least 46,000 judicial and financial offices in the kingdom.[6] No area of royal administration and public services was untouched by venality; and although Colbert, for whom the estimate of 1664 was made, had dreamed of eliminating or at least severely curtailing it, like so many of his plans this one was aborted by the demands of war.[7] Hostilities against the Dutch in the 1670s brought renewed recourse to the easiest form of borrowing yet devised; and the rapacious *traitants* and *partisans*, who were one of the main butts of La Bruyère's disenchanted reflections on the contemporary scene, proved inexhaustible in devising new means of extracting money from what Charles Loyseau had called in 1610 Frenchmen's archomania – their rage for offices.[8] With the quarter-century of almost uninterrupted warfare that began in 1688 these expedients proliferated as never before. Well over 600 *traités* for the creation or exploitation of venal offices were concluded with *partisans* between 1689 and 1715,[9] and by 1710 a capital of over 200 millions had been raised through squeezing office-holders in various ways.[10] And although by 1719 the Regency government was claiming that new offices to the value of over 254 millions had been suppressed since 1711,[11] the net result of Louis XIV's manipulation of venality was a marked increase on the 1664 total

not gained through merit.

of offices. Half a century later, in the year of Voltaire's death, it was estimated at 51,000, and might well have been higher. It represented a capital debt of almost 585 millions.[12]

Venality, therefore, remained a central feature of French society and institutions, throughout Voltaire's lifetime. It was also one remarkably unchallenged, considering its obvious disadvantages.[13] As far back as Plato and Aristotle the sale of public offices had been condemned as setting a higher value on wealth than on virtue. The sale of judicial offices had been bitterly criticised in France throughout the whole period of its expansion, as likely to lead to the sale of justice itself, and to allow moneyed incompetents to sit in judgement over their fellows. But by the eighteenth century such criticism was not much heard. Not a single work appears to have been entirely devoted to the subject: and the handful of writers who did discuss it tended to do so only tangentially. It is true that hardly any of them defended it, but then practices so well-established scarcely needed defending. Above all, was it even worth discussing something that everybody recognised there was no prospect of ever eliminating? The capital invested in offices was equivalent to about a year of the king's gross revenues,[14] too much to even dream of paying back. Although it was the source of almost all the disorders in the administration of justice, reflected Chancellor d'Aguesseau in 1727, to abolish venality was impossible.[15] It was an abuse, but an ineradicable one.

જી

This was the burden of Voltaire's first public comments on the matter. Since leaving school and renouncing the family name, he had had little to do with the world of venality as he pursued a literary career. He was proud of avoiding it. As he boasted to his friend d'Argenson in 1739:

As I had slender means when I entered the great world, I had the insolence to think that I might have an office like anyone else, were it to be acquired by work and by honest effort. I threw myself into the fine arts which always carry with them a certain air of lowness given that they give no exemptions, and that they do not make a man counsellor of the king in his councils. One is a Master of Requests with money, but with money one does not write an epic poem; which is what I did.[16]

But when, in the mid-1740s, he began to achieve official recognition, he found that even the rewards of merit had a price. If the patronage of the king's mistress procured for the newly appointed Historiographer Royal the further post of Gentleman of the Bedchamber at the end of 1746, this latter post was a venal one. Voltaire later boasted of being allowed to sell it for 53,000 *livres* in 1749 but neglected to record what he had had to pay for it in the first place.[17] There was no sign of self-disgust over this foray into the venal labyrinth: rather, a certain pride at the profit realised. Thus it is no surprise to find compromise with the world as it is the theme of one of Voltaire's earliest *contes*, written at precisely this time.

Published in the first collected edition of his works in 1748, *Le monde comme il va* is the story of Babouc, a stranger in Persepolis – a thinly-veiled Paris. At first he is horrified by the absurd customs he finds there. They include young sons of rich fathers buying the right to dispense justice like some piece of land. It seems obvious to him that the sale of verdicts must follow. Nor is he convinced when a young soldier who has bought a command vaunts the virtues of paying to be shot at. Surely, Babouc tells a man of letters, judges should be recruited from mature and experienced jurisconsults rather than raw youths. If young men can command successful armies, comes the reply, there is no reason why they should not prove to be successful magistrates, too. And later, in court, Babouc observes that while mature and learned advocates haver and equivocate, young judges reach swift and fair conclusions based on reason rather than on book learning. 'Babouc concluded that there were often very good things in abuses', for after all, 'if all is not good, it is all passable.'

Tolerant resignation was also the tone of remarks on venality in the *Siècle de Louis XIV*, published in 1751 after almost 20 years of drafts and polishing. The financial *affaires extraordinaires* of the great king's last years (and Voltaire's own adolescence) were described less in a spirit of censure on a government that had created so many ridiculous and superfluous offices, than in a spirit of amusement at the vain folly of those who had bought them for the tax-exemptions they conferred. No doubts were left that in principle venality was bad. We smile today at such things, says the historian, but at the time men wept. And Colbert, earlier, comes in for rare criticism for allowing the extension in the 1670s of what he had set out intending to abolish for ever, venal expedients which burdened future ages for short-term gains. By 1708, however, Colbert's nephew Desmaretz recognised that he 'could not cure an evil which everything rendered incurable'.[18]

The true error was to have introduced it in the first place. Elsewhere Voltaire blamed Francis I for that – the usual culprit – and sometimes Louis XII.[19] But if circumstances made the evil incurable, there was at least no excuse for claiming it had advantages. Accordingly as he grew older, and his view of the world darkened, Voltaire devoted increasing efforts to attacking those who found saving virtues in the sale of offices. Only two important writers in his time attempted to do so, but he took issue with them both. One of them he also believed to be an impostor.

This was the author of the *Testament politique* of Cardinal Richelieu, first published in 1688. Its authenticity was much contested right from the start, but Voltaire only appears to have become interested in the question in the late 1730s, as he began to reflect seriously on the history of the previous century.[20]

Chapter 4 of the *Testament* was a sustained defence of the venality and heredity of offices, but Voltaire's first doubts about its authenticity, expressed in *Conseils à un journaliste* (1737) made no mention of that. Only in 1739 did it come to seem one more reason for believing that the *Testament* could not be by a minister who earlier in his career had been a vocal critic of the sale of offices. What concentrated his mind on this aspect was his reading of d'Argenson's manuscript *Considérations sur le gouvernement ancien et présent de la France*, where venality was identified as the central defect of French government, and one of which Richelieu could never have approved.[21] Voltaire thanked his old friend for adding a further reason for doubting the *Testament's* authenticity, and delighted in his condemnation of an 'unfortunate invention which has deprived citizens of emulation, and which has deprived kings of the throne's finest prerogative'.[22] It is true that the defence of venality was not among the reasons given for doubting the *Testament's* authenticity in the first major piece which he devoted to the subject in 1749;[23] nor is the matter raised in what has since been recognised as the definitive refutation of Voltaire's doubts by Foncemagne, the next year.[24] But when in 1764 a new edition of the *Testament* appeared, together with further observations by Foncemagne, Voltaire returned to the charge with new arguments. 'I know not,' he wrote in the *Doutes nouveaux sur le testament attribué au cardinal de Richelieu,* 'if it be very likely that a great minister should advise perpetuation of the abuse of venality of offices: France is the only country sullied by this disgrace.' Everywhere else in Europe, he noted, magistrates were chosen from the bar: and even in Turkey, Persia and China it was not possible to buy the right to judge men as if it were a meadow or field. No minister could have advised the retention of a 'shameful traffic against which the entire universe cries out'. Even those who had bought judicial offices in France would surely have preferred to have been elected.[25] The sharpening of tone is audible: this was the Voltaire of the 1760s, optimistic illusions all gone, anxious to crush the world's infamies; many of which, in that decade, he found to be perpetrated by the venal magistracy of the parlements.

The other defender of venality with whom he took issue was Montesquieu, who, in a few brief lines of Book V of *De l'esprit des lois*, argued that venality was good in monarchies 'because it makes men do, as a family craft, what they would not undertake out of virtue'.[26] If offices were not publicly sold, courtiers would sell them privately; and in any case, industry would be stimulated if advancement came only from wealth. These arguments, which seem to have owed a good deal in their turn to Richelieu's *Testament*, predictably outraged Voltaire. He had never liked Montesquieu, or his sprawling, unpolished masterpiece; and in the eighth part of *Questions sur l'Encyclopédie* he expressed incredulity that an expedient born of Francis I's financial improvidence could ever be thought good.[27] If it was so good, why had no other country adopted it? 'The monster was born from the prodigality of a king grown indigent, and from the vanity of a few burghers whose fathers had money. This infamous abuse has always been attacked with powerless cries, because offices sold would need to be reimbursed.'

To sell justice, and the right to dispense it, was sacrilegiously vile; and so 'Let us complain that Montesquieu dishonoured his work by such paradoxes. But forgive him. His uncle had bought a provincial office of president, and left it to him. Human nature is everywhere. None of us is without weakness.'

Montesquieu had been dead 16 years when these strictures appeared; but his arguments about the nature of monarchy were never more urgent than in 1771, as Chancellor Maupeou launched his attack on the parlements, which Montesquieu had identified as one of the vital intermediary powers which prevented monarchy from degenerating into despotism. In this confrontation Voltaire,

1771 - Maupeou.

Parlement & venality – Voltaire on Maupeou.

alone among the *philosophes*, unequivocally took the chancellor's side.[28] In the *causes célèbres* which he had espoused in the 1760s – Calas, Sirven, La Barre, Lally – the forces of cruelty, fanaticism and intolerance had always been embodied in the parlements, proud corporations made invulnerable by the tenure derived from venality. These cases occurred during years of deteriorating relations between the king and his sovereign courts, and Voltaire made little secret of his sympathy with the royal side.[29] Only action by the king, he believed, could reform the complex of abuses which they stood for. Awareness of his attitude seems to have brought encouragement from the newly-appointed Chancellor Maupeou to write against the parlements and their pretensions.[30] The result, in 1769, was the *Histoire du Parlement de Paris.* Ostensibly (from the title page) by an 'Abbé de Big...' its authorship was an open secret from the start,[31] and its sentiments towards its subject came as no surprise. The parlement was allowed some merit for its long resistance to the claims of the church, and its support for the king at crucial moments, as in the reign of Henry IV, but its long record of excessive political ambition and judicial savagery was left to speak for itself; and in chapter XVI the basis of its members' tenure was unequivocally condemned. Francis I's chancellor Duprat had 'prostituted' the magistracy when he had auctioned 20 new offices of counsellor, but from this shameful start, which the parlement had at first tried to resist, venality had rapidly spread throughout the judiciary. 'A tax levied equally, and for which town councils and even financiers would have paid out cash, would have been more reasonable and more useful; but the minister was counting on the eagerness of burghers, whose vanity would buy these new offices at every opportunity.' Venality was also condemned as one source of the troubles of the Fronde.[32]

As first published, the *Histoire* ended with the savage execution of Damiens, who had stabbed Louis XV in 1757. Only the dramatic events of the next few years led Voltaire to add two new chapters to later editions.[33] But 1769 also saw the publication of a new edition of the *Précis du Siècle de Louis XV*, which had grown out of earlier prolongations of *Louis XIV*. It contained a long chapter on the laws, largely inspired by Voltaire's reading of Beccaria, but ending with a resounding condemnation of the venality so speciously defended in the *Testament* (which he persisted in believing to be the work of the Abbé Bourzeis).

> In vain have other authors, more courtiers than citizens, and more inspired by personal interest than by love of their country[34] followed behind the Abbé Bourzeys; a proof that this sale is an abuse, is that it was only brought about by another abuse, that is through the dissipation of the finances of the State. It is a simony far more fatal than the sale of church benefices: for if an isolated ecclesiastic buys a simple benefice, the result is neither good nor bad for the country, where he has no jurisdiction, he is answerable to nobody; but magistracy has the honour, the fortune and the life of men in its hands. We are seeking in this century to perfect everything, so let us seek to perfect the laws.

The reforms of Maupeou in 1771 seemed to present an ideal opportunity for such improvement. For all the stormy exchanges between the king and his parlements throughout the 1760s, Maupeou's attack on the sovereign courts was not premeditated, and the radical form it eventually took developed out of the crisis itself.[35] But from the start of the confrontation Voltaire, as he told d'Alembert and Richelieu on 21 December 1770, was pleased to see the murderers of La Barre humiliated.[36] His pleasure grew over the spring of 1771 as Maupeou, unable to conciliate or cow the Parlement of Paris, embarked on a radical restructuring of the upper judiciary. Most of the members of the parlement were dismissed, and their offices confiscated, although compensation was promised. They were replaced by salaried nominees, who were forbidden to charge litigants the traditional fees (*épices*). At the same time the vast jurisdiction of the parlement was broken up and redistributed among a number of superior councils, staffed and operating on the same terms. Maupeou even encouraged hopes of a total recodification of the law. Voltaire was overwhelmed at the promise of it all. 'I admit to you,' he wrote to Florian on 1 April,[37] 'that I clap my hands, when I see that justice is no longer venal, that citizens are no longer dragged from the dungeons of Angoulême to the dungeons of the Conciergerie...I say it out loud, this regulation appears to me the finest ever made since the foundation of the monarchy; and I think one would have to be an enemy of the State and of oneself not to feel the benefit.'

It is clear that ending the sale of offices was only one of several reasons why Voltaire supported the chancellor's policies, and perhaps not the most important. It certainly did not figure largely in the arguments of the eight pamphlets he wrote in favour of the reforms between March and May 1771. As early as the end of January he had sent Maupeou indirect evidence of his support,[38] and the chancellor can only have welcomed his satirising the constitutional doctrines of the parlements,[39] his response to Malesherbes' great remonstrances against his policies on behalf of the Court of Aids,[40] and a number of other fleeting though anonymous interventions. But the sale of offices was attacked more specifically in revised editions of earlier works published during the years of Maupeou's ministry, and in ongoing serial publications such as *Questions sur l'Encyclopédie*. The entry '*Loix, Esprit des Loix*', of 1771, cited above, was one. The next year, in the ninth part, came an entry specifically on venality. Beginning with yet another attack on the authenticity of Richelieu's *Testament politique*, it argued that Maupeou had at last given the lie to the strongest argument there advanced in favour of venality – that the system was simply too expensive to buy out.

> And so, not only did this abuse seem to all the world irreformable, but useful; men were so accustomed to this disgrace, that they no longer felt it; it seemed eternal; a single man was able in a few months to wipe it out. Let us then repeat that anything can be done, anything be corrected; that the great defect of almost all who govern, is to have only half a will and half the means.[41]

This was to attribute too much to Maupeou. Only in the parlements and certain other courts suppressed in his reforms was venality abolished: perhaps 3,500 venal offices out of over 50,000. The salaries of the new non-venal magistracy, and the free justice that resulted were paid for by earmarked tax increases. Maupeou's colleague at the finance ministry, indeed, the Abbé Terray, introduced a range of measures in 1771 which positively extended venality in some areas and taxed it more ruthlessly at every level. So far from diminishing it, the aim was to make it pay better. As most of the other *philosophes* saw, in fact, Maupeou's reforms were largely cosmetic.[42] What they saw in him was a friend of the Jesuits, Mme Dubarry's sycophant, and a supporter of stricter censorship. His attack on the sovereign courts had swept away the only legal safeguards enjoyed by the king's subjects, and turned that king into a despot. In this perspective, venality, insofar as it reinforced the independence of the judiciary, had been a positive bulwark of liberty: as Diderot put it, an evil, but a necessary one.[43]

Voltaire never recognised any of this. Even though Maupeou, once his system established itself, showed himself indifferent to a number of causes espoused by Voltaire,[44] and forbade publication of new parts of the *Questions sur l'Encyclopédie* in France, and even though no official support was received for securing a performance of his last, sycophantic play, *Les Lois de Minos*, in Paris, much less for the long-coveted permission to return to the city of his birth, Voltaire nevertheless remained a champion of the judicial reforms until they were abrogated by a new king in 1774. This time he took no public stance on the changes, although privately he lamented the restoration of the old Parlement of Paris, its swollen jurisdiction, and the fact that it was to be 'smeared again' (*rebarbouillé*) by venality of offices.[45] But when, the next year, he brought out a further edition of the *Histoire du Parlement*, there was a new final chapter justifying the work of Maupeou by a recital of the 'astonishing anarchy' and judicial cruelties that had marked the 1760s, and of the utility of two reforms that the chancellor had introduced. One was the diminution of the 'ruinous' size of the parlement's jurisdiction. The other was the ending of venality, 'At once shameful and expensive...venality which brought in the high level of fees.' The new parlement 'would be paid by the king, without buying offices, and without demanding anything from litigants...the disgrace of venality, with which unfortunately Francis I and chancellor Duprat sullied France, was washed away by Louis XV and by the efforts of chancellor Maupeou'. After that, few could doubt the real meaning of the terse praise for Louis XVI's restoration of the old order with which the chapter concluded.

And Voltaire continued to rail against venality until the end. 1777 saw the publication of his *Commentaire sur quelques maximes de l'Esprit des lois*, in which, after a little grudging initial praise for Montesquieu, he proceeded to challenge some of his central principles. The passage on venality was inevitably targeted, although most of Voltaire's remarks were nearly word for word the same as those in *Questions sur l'Encyclopédie*. Montesquieu's contention that a vice like venality could be a virtue in monarchy was unworthy of him. 'Why was this strange abuse only introduced at the close of eleven hundred years?' And appropriately, he combined these last comments on one of his secular aversions with a jibe at the church: 'This abuse has always been attacked with powerless cries, because offices sold would have to be reimbursed. It would have been a thousand times better, says a wise jurisconsult, to sell the treasure of all the monasteries and the plate of all the churches than to sell justice.'

❧

It seemed an implicit suggestion that venality could be bought out with the confiscated wealth of the church – and that is how it was eventually done. Only 11 years after Voltaire died venality was abolished, and free justice proclaimed by the National Assembly on the night of 4 August 1789. Office-holders were promised reimbursement of their investment, and this obligation was recognised as part of the national debt. By the end of the year the Assembly had confiscated the lands of the church as a means of paying off that debt.[46]

No doubt the writings of Voltaire played their part in sowing the seeds of these developments, but not in any directly demonstrable sense. He was merely the most famous of a myriad of writers who attacked the church and the ways of the established judicial system, and thereby helped to undermine respect for both. And in the case of venality he was saying nothing new. The arguments he used were as old as venality itself. The first evidence for its existence came from the protests of medieval estates against the sale of judicial offices,[47] and they had been much reiterated in the sixteenth and seventeenth centuries. The importance of Voltaire's contribution lay not in the novelty of what he said, but in the fact that he was saying it. He scarcely mentioned the matter publicly until he was a writer of international standing. And when he did address it, most often he did so in order to refute authoritative figures who advanced new defences of the indefensible. Richelieu's authority was much more effectively challenged when it was Voltaire who declared that it was not Richelieu's at all: Montesquieu's when his fellow academician

+ Confiscated, ecclesial lands to pay off venal debts.

claimed his judgement had been warped by self-interest. Here Voltaire lent his prestige to the silent common sense of his compatriots, whose disapproval of venality came out loud and clear when they had the opportunity to voice an opinion in the *cahiers* of 1789.[48]

Yet the venality condemned by Voltaire made up only one small part of the system, and until the 1760s he had condemned it with no great vehemence. On the venality amid which he had grown up, and in which he had himself briefly dabbled in the 1740s, he remained silent. His fiercest attacks were concentrated almost entirely on the venal tenure of magistrates whom, in the course of the 1760s, he had come to hate and despise for other reasons. It is clear from his private correspondence that he supported Maupeou largely because he had struck down the murderers of La Barre and Lally. The chancellor's other reforms, including the curtailing of venality, merely confirmed how right it was to support such a minister. Fundamentally, however, they were side issues.

They were side issues for Maupeou, too, although the cruelty and obscurantism of the magistracy were of no concern to him. Reform of the judiciary was merely a screen to give respectability to his own political ambition. Once firmly established, he did not pursue it; nothing came of the vaunted law-code which so excited Voltaire, and outside the parlements venality was left untouched, though not untaxed. But meanwhile, all restraints on despotism, of which venal tenure was one, had been swept aside. The other *philosophes* saw this, and found their doyen's support for the chancellor an embarrassment. In his obsession with avenging injustice, the patriarch of Ferney seemed to have forgotten about protecting liberty. Babouc no longer recognised that some abuses could be very good things. Most opinion, however, did so; and until the threat of despotism was banished in 1789, the memory of Maupeou's reforms helped to prop up the very venality which Voltaire had praised them so highly for trying to abolish.

CHAPTER 3

Secular Simony: The Clergy and the Sale of Offices in Eighteenth-Century France

" Simony "

Aversion to the sale of its own authority is one of the oldest established principles of the Christian church. Ever since St. Peter rebuked the sorcerer Simon Magus for attempting to buy spiritual powers from the apostles,[1] it has been axiomatic that priesthood and cure of souls may not be acquired for money. Yet, once benefices became entitlements to remuneration, the offence to which Simon gave his name became endemic in the church. The frequency with which councils, popes, bishops, and divines condemned simony shows how persistent it was, and in the early modern church it incurred the particular censure of the Council of Trent.[2]

An even older tradition, going back at least as far as Plato and Aristotle,[3] condemns the sale of public office. The powers of the magistrate rank second only in scope and importance to those of the priest, and their exercise requires qualities that no money can buy. Unlike the Christian condemnation of simony, the critique of venality derived not from authority but from principles of reason and justice. It was no less pointed for that. The sale, whether covert or overt, of public functions goes back as far as civil society itself – as once again the antiquity, number and persistence of its critics show. Despite all their strictures, by the later Middle Ages the roots of civil venality were as deep as those of simony in the church, and just as resistant to extirpation. In parts of early modern Europe, selling offices became the open and established practice of government at a time when it was easier to sell rich men honours than to tax them. Nowhere did it spread more widely than in France, where between the sixteenth and the eighteenth centuries all but a handful of public officials were recruited by purchase. It took a revolution to uproot this system. Even then vestiges of it survived, and survive still, though periodically denounced in arguments first heard several centuries before Christ.[4]

The practices of the church were not unconnected with the development of French secular venality. The very definition of an office, when it solidified in an ordinance of 1467, had obvious parallels with an ecclesiastical benefice. It was defined as an appointment tenable for life. Its holder could be removed only by death, forfeiture, or resignation.[5] One reason why the sale of offices flourished in France was that from an early stage their holders enjoyed almost free disposal of their purchase to third parties. Not only did the king sell offices; he allowed buyers to sell them on, or to bequeath them to their own heirs. It was done through a *resignatio in favorem*, a conditional resignation, the condition being that a designated successor was provided. These instruments had first been developed for the transfer of ecclesiastical benefices in the gift of the pope, and they offered some of the most obvious opportunities for simony. Adapted for the transfer of French royal offices, the commercial purpose was undisguised. Only one constraint limited the free disposal of incumbents who resigned ecclesiastical benefices conditionally. If they died within 20 days of doing so, disposal reverted to the provisor.[6] In the 1530s a similar rule was introduced for French royal offices.[7] Offices conditionally resigned reverted to the crown if the officer resigning died within 40 days. Insurance against this eventuality was the attraction of

⟶ Annuel.

the *droit annuel* or *paulette* introduced in 1604, and destined to be the most effective and durable way of taxing venal office-holders.

The laws governing French venality were therefore deeply marked by the ways of the church. This did not prevent the clergy, through their representatives in successive Estates-General, from taking a lead throughout the sixteenth century in denouncing the seemingly inexorable spread of the practice.[8] Among the most vocal of their spokesmen in the Estates-General of 1614, the last to convene before the Revolution, was Richelieu, and in the early years of his ministry a decade later this prince of the church advised Louis XIII to undertake the entire abolition of the sale and heredity of offices,[9] By the time he died, however, the cardinal had concluded that any such attempt would be difficult, if not positively dangerous. He admitted that the general opinion of mankind, as well as reason and the best legal principles, were opposed to venality and heredity. But, 'in an ancient Monarchy, whose imperfections have grown into habits, and whose disorder forms (not uselessly) part of the order of the State',[10] it was better to let well-established ways and institutions continue, until better men in a better age could undertake their reform with wisdom and safety. As a minister, Richelieu had come to know how the judicious exploitation of office-holders and their ambitions and appetites could help the state pursue its own. And, although these opinions did not become known until the publication of the cardinal's *Testament politique* in 1688, only Colbert among his ministerial successors thought that venality could be much curtailed. Richelieu's was to be the conventional wisdom of the eighteenth century, echoed and endorsed by Montesquieu: venality was ineradicable, and had some advantages. It was a necessary evil.

Confidence in the permanence of venality meant that venal offices retained their appeal throughout the eighteenth century. On the eve of the Revolution, many categories were more sought-after than ever, as rising prices testified.[11] A small but distinctive sector of the system was that of clerical counsellorships in the parlements. In medieval times clerics occupied a whole range of royal offices from which they would later be excluded,[12] but the parlements retained a handful of offices specifically reserved for clergy. When, under Francis I, the sale of offices in the parlements became avowed royal policy, no exception was made for clerical counsellors. Although holders of these offices were required to be in holy orders, they were still required to pay, and their purchase was not deemed simoniacal. The only concession to the cloth of clerical counsellors was that they were excused from sitting on cases whose outcome might involve the shedding of blood, and so avoided service in the *tournelles* or criminal chambers of these courts. Whereas a large provincial parlement like Bordeaux had only six clerical counsellors in the eighteenth century, in Paris there were 12.[13] But not all these offices were occupied by clerics. Royal dispensations from major orders, or even any priestly qualifications at all, were easily obtained.[14] In 1725, four of the six clerical posts in the Bordeaux parlement were held by laymen.[15] There seems, in fact, to have been limited competition among properly qualified candidates. A new clerical counsellorship created in the Parlement of Besançon in 1704 failed to find a buyer, and four years later was laicised;[16] and prices for these charges throughout the kingdom tended to be markedly lower than for lay counsellorships.[17]

It is not difficult to understand why. Even if a cleric could afford an office, he lacked the layman's incentive of children to pass it on to. The higher age of entry of most clerical counsellors[18] also suggests that a legal career might be a last resort, when other hopes of preferment had faded. The typical clerical counsellor was a younger son from a family already represented in the same court. These offices enabled well-born priests of modest means to establish themselves with dignity in positions that reflected well on their families. Remuneration for service in a parlement was unspectacular,[19] but an assiduous counsellor would find it a useful supplement to other resources. Besides, being a member of the parlement could bring additional advancement in the church. In Paris, at least, where the king needed political support inside the court, assiduity could be rewarded with benefices in the royal gift. Most clerical counsellors in the capital had prebends or stalls in well-endowed chapters, and a score of them were commendatory abbots, often in several houses.[20] Two even went on to be appointed bishops.[21] For those achieving ecclesiastical preferment in this way, purchase of an office was a sort of simony at one remove, but without the stigma.

To become a bishop, however (unless one of those deemed a peer, with rights of session), was to move outside the parlement, which few established clerical counsellors ever did. They were indeed among the longest serving of magistrates.[22] When they moved on, it was more by chance than from expectation. Thus it was an old friendship with the family of Mme de Pompadour which brought the Abbé de Salaberry promotion, at 61, to one of the ecclesiastical seats on the Council of State in 1758. When he died, three years later, he was succeeded there by the Abbé Bertin, of the Parlement of Bordeaux, brother as it happened to the comptroller-general of the finances.[23] The most famous (or notorious) success story was that of the Abbé Terray, who in 1769 became comptroller-general himself. His promotion, after 33 years in the parlement, caused universal surprise, but perhaps should not have. He owed it to Chancellor Maupeou, with whom he had worked closely in the parlement throughout the mid-1760s. Maupeou had then been prime president, and Terray *rapporteur de la cour*.

Here was one position, not an office, to which a clerical counsellor in Paris might legitimately aspire, since it traditionally went to one of them. Salaberry had been Terray's predecessor, and only once subsequently between 1781 and 1785, was the *rapporteur* a lay counsellor, much to the outrage of all the clerics.[24] The responsibilities of the *rapporteur* were heavy. In co-operation with the procurator-general he was required to present and explain legislation sent by the king for registration in the parlement. Considerable abilities and tactical sense were required, and, as the government's financial difficulties deepened over the century, the demands of the post grew ever more daunting. When in 1785 it was recaptured for the clerics by the Abbé Tandeau, it was reputedly with the inducement of an abbacy worth 25,000 *livres* a year.[25] These duties provided a very effective training for the formulation, understanding and conduct of high policy, as Terray went on to demonstrate; but no doubt his ruthless and extortionate record in power helped to ensure that no subsequent clerical counsellor was offered the chance to emulate him.

The original rationale of having clerical counsellors in the parlements was to safeguard the legal interests of the church. Worldly men of business like Salaberry, Terray, or Tandeau in the eighteenth century devoted little enough of their time or energies to that. It largely became the monopoly of those who took a distinctive view of the church's interests, seeing them as under fundamental threat from everything to do with *Unigenitus*. Although most of the identifiable Jansenists within the Parlement of Paris were laymen,[26] there was a core of clerical counsellors down the generations, from the Abbé Purcelle, who led the early opposition to the Bull under the Regency, or his ally the Abbé de Guillebauld, to men like the Abbés Chauvelin or Nigon de Berty, who came to prominence when the quarrels were rekindled in mid-century by the refusal of sacraments.[27] Placed as they were in the premier court of the kingdom, these men were sometimes able to play a crucial role in politics, as when Chauvelin launched the parlement's great attack on the Jesuits in 1761.[28] And, whether or not he was acting on that famous occasion as the agent, or puppet of deeper forces, his status as a cleric lent authority to his denunciation.

It is true that at the time, and since, doubts were raised about how sincere a Jansenist Chauvelin was, if indeed he was one at all.[29] Jansenism always flourished behind a fog of denials and dubious attributions. Sincere 'friends of the truth' in the parlement, however, had the very basis of their power questioned by one of the leading Jansenist writers on politics when his most important posthumous work appeared in 1739. The Abbé Jacques-Joseph Duguet, sometime priest of the Oratory, had written his *Institution d'un prince* in 1699,[30] perhaps in response to the literary sensation caused by the appearance of Richelieu's *Testament politique*. Certainly it was a comprehensive polemic against the practices and instruments of French absolutism, including the surrender of authority by kings to ministers. But Duguet never allowed its publication during his lifetime. Too much of it was scarcely veiled criticism of Louis XIV; and by the time the author died in 1736, another cardinal was exercising the royal authority. Duguet, like most Jansenists, vaunted the role of the parlement in public affairs, and defended the right of remonstrance. He praised the virtues of magistrates bred from generations on the bench. But he denounced the sale of judicial offices as a 'disorder contrary to Justice' leading to excessive costs. Princes had a duty to bring an end to both.[31]

Duguet's denunciation of venality was sustained and impassioned. The sale of judicial offices meant that only the rich and presumptuous ever became magistrates, whereas the best princes had always preferred to appoint men who shunned authority. Since the highest duty of the prince was to choose the men who would sit in judgement over his subjects, it was a prerogative which should never be alienated – least of all for reasons of transient financial need, which left a permanent burden of debt for the state. In a series of rhetorical questions which recalled a sermon, Duguet reviewed the evils of selling the right to judge. Since when had riches been a proof of integrity, knowledge or a zeal for justice? Was all wealth virtuously acquired? What would become of impecunious men of virtue and talent, and what sort of example was it that their qualities should be left to languish 'in dust and oblivion'? 'Where will be striving for fine things, if Riches alone are the gateway to all Employments?'[32] And would not those who had bought the power of justice also sell it? Venality forced men of good birth and background from the bench, replacing them with 'new men, obscure, nameless, without connections, without elevation, without courage' for whom the public would have no respect. When magistracy was venal, greed became the measure of all things; and even in respectable families necessary investment in offices immobilised capital and warped inheritance. Above all, however, a venal magistracy meant that the dispensation of justice was the only profession needing neither ability, aptitude, nor knowledge, when none demanded these qualities more. Who would employ a doctor, or even a humble artisan, or servant, solely on the basis of his or her wealth? Money was the enemy of all virtue and public good.

Nor did Duguet accept (responding most obviously in this to the recently revealed arguments of Richelieu) that 'if evil it be... it is henceforth without remedy; and time should not be lost in deploring it fruitlessly'. On the contrary, 'it is impossible that a Prince, moved by this disorder and its fatal results, should not seek for remedies without yielding to difficulties which seem insurmountable'.[33] He accepted the injustice of outright abolition or confiscation of offices that had become property. Their holders would need to be reimbursed. Nor would it be just to buy them out at the original, often remote, selling price. A fixed 'milieu' should be established, and declared permanent and invariable, and at this price the prince would pay off office-holders 'by degrees'.

Those reimbursed would be replaced by nominees where necessary; but since the over-proliferation of judges through venality was, in Duguet's opinion, one of the main causes of the high costs of justice, not all of those bought out would have successors.

A quarter of a century after Duguet wrote, but the same length of time before his treatise was finally published, another clerical writer also addressed the problem of judicial costs. Anxious to rehabilitate himself after public criticism of the scarcely cold Louis XIV had brought his expulsion from the French Academy in 1718, in 1725 the Abbé de Saint-Pierre published a *Mémoire pour diminuer le nombre des procès*. In his view, a wide range of factors had made the French litigious and kept the costs of justice high, but venality was undoubtedly one among them. Jurisdictions had proliferated in order that offices might be sold within them, and all investors in office expected a return. And nobody could disagree that to award judicial office to the highest bidder irrespective of capacity was 'highly inconvenient'.[34] Yet Saint-Pierre, too, had obviously read Richelieu, and he repeated the argument, which the cardinal claimed first to have heard from Sully, that venality had saved France from a judiciary recruited from among the clients and retainers of powerful magnates.[35] Other things being equal, it was better, argued Saint-Pierre (this time echoing Aristotle[36]) that rich men rather than poor should be judges, since their wealth placed them beyond corruption. Most important was that appointment should depend not on wealth alone. Prices should be held at modest levels, so that there was no shortage of candidates among whom members of a venal company should then choose by election. 'And so I am for venality, provided it be carried on within just limits, but its price should be modest, so that among aspirants there be all at once riches, emulation, competition, and a choice of Magistrates among candidates.'[37]

Saint-Pierre, a worldly cleric, proto-*philosophe* and polymath, had little in common with the austere Duguet. He was equally remote from perhaps the best-known churchman to write on public affairs in the eighteenth century, Fénelon. Though no Jansenist, like Duguet the archbishop of Cambrai was moved to write by what he saw as the unbridled excesses of a monarch obsessed by wars and glory. And, as with Duguet, his more extreme pronouncements did not become public until after his death. Appearing fleetingly as an appendix to a rapidly suppressed edition of *Télémaque* in 1734, his *Lettre à Louis XIV* of c.1702, and *Examen de conscience sur les devoirs de la royauté*, prepared for the Duke of Burgundy in 1711, became generally available only in 1747.[38] In both, Fénelon concentrated his attack on the over-proliferation of venality rather than the thing itself. By over-creation of offices to sell, Louis XIV had burdened posterity with perpetual debts, only repayable at ruinous cost to the taxpayer. He had pushed up the costs of justice through the greed of office-buyers to recoup their outlay at the people's expense. He had, indeed, destabilised the entire good order of the state by making most functions venal monopolies. Justice was now more venal, reform increasingly impossible. Ten years of funding wars by such expedients had done damage that might take centuries to repair.[39] Nowhere did Fénelon suggest the entire abandonment of venality, although he advised the Duke of Burgundy to abolish it in the army, and suppress hundreds of special jurisdictions whose members were recruited by purchase. He advocated the gradual elimination of the *paulette*, and the expulsion from the royal councils of masters of requests 'brought in without merit for money'.[40] Here Fénelon's contempt for the very principle of venality came through clearly enough. But, like Richelieu, he appears to have believed that there was little prospect of eliminating it entirely, even under the model king he hoped Burgundy would be.

In this, his writings when they appeared underscored the conventional wisdom of the eighteenth century. Over the last century of its existence the sale and heredity of public offices in France found no more defenders than it ever had.[41] But the issue provoked no public debate, because the impossibility of eliminating it entirely was taken for granted. The most anybody dared suggest was ways to trim it, while disagreements largely centred on whether this public malady had any redeeming features. Clerical writers were as divided on these questions as any, but Duguet was alone in believing the evil eradicable. He appears to have persuaded nobody else, but his attack was resounding enough to have alarmed a man with more to lose from the abolition of venality than anybody else. Louis-Auguste Bertin was treasurer-general of the Parts Casual, the bureau from which most of the venal system was administered. He was, perhaps unsurprisingly, the only person in this whole century to mount an unequivocal public defence of the sale of offices.[42] And in a private manuscript dictionary of offices he picked out Duguet by name as a misguided critic to be refuted.[43]

Interestingly, none of the clerical writers who discussed venality drew the parallel with simony. It was left to Voltaire to make that connection, characteristically to disparage both. Venality was worse than simony, he observed in a late edition of the *Précis du siècle de Louis XV*, because selling judicial authority placed the lives and livelihoods of citizens in potentially incompetent hands. Buying ecclesiastical benefices had no such concrete and practical consequences.[44]

Few clerics would have agreed that simony was so harmless, even if it had not implied agreeing with an opinion of Voltaire. But it was not merely a handful of clerical writers who condemned or criticised the sale of public offices. When they were given the opportunity to pronounce publicly on the state of the kingdom, the eighteenth-century French clergy as a whole yielded nothing to their sixteenth and seventeenth-century predecessors in their denunciation of venality and its consequences. As in earlier centuries, their opportunity came with the convocation of the Estates-General and the drawing up of *cahiers* to guide the deliberations of chosen deputies. All bishops and parish priests, and elected representatives from the capitular and regular clergy, participated in the electoral assemblies which produced these *cahiers*, of which 158 survive.[45] A survey of 150, therefore, gives a uniquely full picture of clerical opinion on the eve of the Revolution.

When Richelieu had been young the introduction of overt venality by Francis I was still just within living memory, and it remained possible to hope that its advance might yet be curbed. What is remarkable in the clerical *cahiers* of 1789 is that, even after two further centuries during which the sale of offices had continued to root itself in almost every corner of public life, it remained in clerical eyes an unacceptable abuse. Not a single clerical *cahier* defended it, although seven (or 4.66 per cent of the total) recognised that it might not be possible to buy out venal public offices entirely. This was a lower proportion than either the third estate (6.34 per cent) or the nobility (9.8 per cent), suggesting a less compromising, or perhaps more utopian, attitude to reform among the clergy. It is true that only ten (6.66 per cent) clerical *cahiers* condemned venality in general, as opposed to 18 noble (11.76 per cent) and 26 (13.75 per cent) third estate. General condemnation, however, did not bulk large in any of the *cahiers*. It was normally condemned in specific contexts, where its disadvantages were demonstrated in practice. Thus 30 clerical *cahiers* denounced judicial venality. The terms used by the clergy of Loudun were typical,[46] with the blend of moral earnestness and practical naivety so characteristic of the spirit of 1789:

> Through a deplorable abuse, riches, almost everywhere supplanting wisdom and sometimes probity, we see with pain that for the most part offices of magistracy are acquired by men who have no other merit than enough money to purchase the right to judge their

fellow citizens; it is a radical vice in our government which causes many ills, but it could be remedied...above all by abolishing, if possible, venality of offices...so that, choosing only among enlightened men of mature age and renowned probity, the scales of justice might no longer incline without discernment or be swayed by passion, since they would be in sure hands.

Eleven clerical *cahiers* also condemned venal ennoblement, but this was a far less immediate preoccupation for clerics than for nobles deploring adulteration (79 *cahiers,* almost 52 per cent) or lay commoners resenting the role of naked wealth in social promotion (46 *cahiers,* 24 per cent). The clergy noticed the effects of venality most when it impinged on the lives of their parishioners. Eight per cent of their *cahiers,* for instance, complained of the depredations of the water and forest tribunals, whose magistrates recouped their outlay in fees levied on country people. 'It is an abuse', declared the clergy of Mantes,[47] 'that masterships of forests and waters give the right to exact sometimes 30, sometimes 36, sometimes 40 sous, and even more, for permitting an individual to cut down a tree which is sometimes not worth that sum.' More clerical *cahiers* evoked this source of grievance than third-estate ones, though not those of the woodland-owning nobility. And if the tax-exempt clergy were much less concerned than the other two orders about the activities of the exceptional courts which enforced the state's fiscal demands, they fully shared their anger at the most deeply felt grievance related to venality to emerge from the *cahiers,* the recently enhanced monopoly of the auctioneer-valuers (*huissiers-priseurs*).[48] These functions had been a venal monopoly in principle since the time of Louis XIV, but in 1780 Necker had authorised a tightening of the monopoly prior to remarketing the offices at a higher price. The result was to flood the kingdom in the years down to 1789 with predatory swarms of officials demanding fees on every form of non-commercial property transfer. Nearly a third of all *cahiers*

(32 per cent) complained about them, including a fifth of all clerical ones.

> Also to be demanded [declared the clergy of Beauvais] is the abolition of the office of auctioneer-valuer newly created by the King. These officers singularly oppress the widow and the orphan, and country folk in general, by subjecting what they inherit to enormous fees which they are in no state to bear, and should this abolition not come about, we ask at least for competition, as it has always been required by lords and high judicial officers[49]

Despite differences of emphasis and concern, in general the clergy of 1789 showed themselves exercised about the same elements in venality as the other two orders. The *cahiers* reveal little specific to clerical opinion. Apart from the question of venal ennoblement, the greatest contrast in emphasis was over compensation to office-holders when venality should be abolished or pruned. The problem of reimbursement had always seemed decisive proof that venality could never be eliminated. Nowhere in the *cahiers* was it ever suggested that it should be abolished or curtailed without compensation. But, whereas 31 per cent of third-estate and 23 per cent of noble *cahiers* insisted that whatever happened the losers must be paid for their losses, only 15 clerical *cahiers*, or 10 per cent, showed any interest in this problem. One at least[50] suggested a solution already helping since 1776 to phase out purchase among army officers – a 25 per cent diminution of price at each successive mutation, eliminating any capital value entirely over four exchanges, but imposing real losses on each successive seller. Were the clergy less concerned than the laity about compensating those who profited from an abuse that must be ended? Or did they fear that to insist on compensation would lead legislators to seek means of funding reimbursement at the church's expense? Voltaire had already hinted that it would be better to sell all church plate than to sell justice.[51] And here and there among the *cahiers* of the two lay orders there were suggestions that ecclesiastical wealth could be used to fund the diminution of venality.[52] If this was the clergy's fear, it was eventually to be realised.

On the night of 4 August 1789, along with many of the social institutions of the ancien régime, venality and heredity of judicial and municipal offices were abolished by the National Assembly.[53] Before the Assembly finally dispersed, that abolition had been extended to all forms of venality. And within days of the first abolition, on 11 August, the principle had been accepted that the Nation would compensate holders of formerly venal offices for their losses. Isolated voices warning of the financial burdens that this would entail were quite drowned out. Nevertheless the problem they raised was real enough. Brought into being by a monarchy no longer able to meet its debts unaided, the representative body that became the National Assembly committed itself from the outset to honouring the state's commitments. Within months, however, it had come to recognise that there was no prospect of doing so without the extraordinary expedient of nationalising the lands of the church to provide a new fund of confidence. The church was to bear the cost of satisfying the Nation's creditors.

In a sense the capital tied up in venal offices was part of the state's funded debt. To abolish them meant repaying it, and the knowledge that this commitment had been made can only have spurred the deputies into their fateful decision to confiscate ecclesiastical wealth. In the event it proved even more costly than most deputies had foreseen, since reimbursing office-holders involved refunding what they had paid to their predecessors rather than simply the capital which the crown had received when offices were first marketed. Eventually the Assembly felt unable to make complete restitution, despite earlier promises. But even then the cost was so high that a massive expansion in the planned quantity of *assignats* issued on the security of former church lands had to be authorised – the first step towards the catastrophic monetary inflation that marked the revolutionary years. Dispossessed clerics could take solace that God had thus punished the Revolution for its plunder of the church; but there was little consolation in the knowledge that so much of their former property was dispersed to liquidate a practice which they had always denounced. Ironically, the only clerics to reap any benefit were that handful who had accepted venality – the clerical counsellors in the parlements, reimbursed in full[54] for the loss of the only positions available for purchase by priests.

Diderot by Jean-Antoine Houdon

CHAPTER 4

Changing Notions of Public Corruption
(*c.*1770–*c.*1850)

The practice of selling public offices, embedded in French social and political practice since the Middle Ages, came abruptly to an end with the French Revolution. And although versions of it reappeared in the early nineteenth century, and exist still in certain corners of French life, after 1789 nobody seriously advocated its formal restoration. That was because it was now generally accepted as corrupt. Purchase was no longer seen as a legitimate or acceptable way of recruiting the wielders of any sort of public authority, whether civil or military.

How and why had this change come about? Obviously the operative factor was the French Revolution, but that explains little in itself. Why had the revolutionaries seen the abolition as such a priority? Venality was among the first institutions of the old regime to be abolished, disappearing with feudalism, tithe, judicial fees and a whole range of other things, now deemed 'abuses', on the night of 4 August 1789. Even more important, perhaps, why did this abolition last? Not everything reformed by the Revolution, after all, stayed reformed, and many of the changes attempted by the revolutionaries would soon enough be openly and deliberately reversed. All this suggests that more profound forces were at work than the opportunistic zeal and crowd psychology of excited deputies on a hot August night.

Nor, probably, were these profounder factors exclusively French. The French revolutionaries loved to see themselves as pioneers setting an example to the rest of the world: the principles they espoused were universal, but France had produced them. French historians of the Revolution have perhaps too often been prepared to accept such claims at face-value. But as a foreigner, initially trained in British history, I was forcibly struck by parallel changes over the same period in the hegemonic values of British public life. Although not without its critics, around 1770 what would soon be called 'Old Corruption' was part and parcel of the way Great Britain was governed. It is true that since the mid-seventeenth century there had been little overt venality in civil and judicial offices in Great Britain (though not none), but purchase was normal for officers in the army, just as it was in France.[1] And influence-peddling through the distribution of jobs, sinecures and pensions was the accepted way in which British governments put together parliamentary majorities. In 1774, in fact, the French philosopher Denis Diderot explicitly compared venality in his own country with the purchase of parliamentary seats in Great Britain. Both seemed to him necessary evils.[2] Three generations later, however, much of this situation had been swept away. Parliament had been reformed, 'Economical Reform' had pruned away hundreds of jobs and sinecures, and military purchase was under sustained attack. The standard analyses of how this came about, by W.D. Rubinstein, and more recently Philip Harling,[3] have analysed these developments almost exclusively in British domestic terms, except for the occasional invocation of the 'spirit of the times', and 'fundamental ideological and cultural reasons' which made the complex of practices called Old Corruption 'increasingly intolerable and unacceptable'.[4] But it is precisely these ideological and cultural factors, transcending individual states, that it seems to me require further investigation.

There is another curious parallel worth noting, too. There was nothing new about most of the arguments deployed to condemn the sale of offices in France, or Old Corruption across the Channel. Condemnations of the role of private wealth and private greed in public affairs go back to the beginnings of western political thought, to Plato and Aristotle.[5] Men of education in early modern times would have been familiar with Plato's principle that the virtue essential for the proper discharge of public business was incompatible with any sort of private gain. And although Aristotle contended that rich men made the best magistrates, that was only because their wealth would place them beyond temptation. In France, the sale of offices had always been denounced as corrupt. Indeed, such denunciations in the Middle Ages are the earliest evidence we have that the practice existed. And what I found in the eighteenth century was that there was little real public debate about venality, because hardly anybody could be found to defend it.[6] If it was discussed at all, it was condemned as self-evidently outrageous. In Great Britain, where one of the functions of parliament had always been to bring the subject's grievances to the attention of the sovereign, there was a long tradition of denouncing the practices which later would be called Old Corruption, as well as a number which had disappeared by the time that term emerged, but were deemed equally corrupt, such as the granting of monopolies under Elizabeth I.[7] And the Economical Reform which in the 1780s began the onslaught on Old Corruption and prompted its definition as such, was rooted in a century of country opposition rhetoric and failed place-bills. Economical Reform, indeed, marked the onset of a culture in which place-bills were no longer doomed to fail. And that, in turn, really encapsulates the problem. Why did principles whose validity had always been widely recognised, but whose force had been ignored, come quite quickly, over not more than two or three generations, to dictate the conduct of public business? How had public corruption been transformed from a necessary evil into an absolute one?

To begin with necessity. Why had Diderot thought venality (which he said he spent every day of his life cursing) and parliamentary corruption *necessary* evils? He gave two reasons. One was the Aristotelian argument that rich men who had invested in public authority would have no need to use it for private profit. And this implied a second consideration. Such men were likely as a result to be more zealous practitioners of public virtue, and defenders of public liberty. What prompted these reflections was the attack in 1771 by Chancellor Maupeou on the French parlements, the sovereign courts of justice who were the main critics of absolute monarchy, and hitherto protected from governmental retribution by the tenure which their members had bought. Maupeou accompanied his attack by suppressing venality in these courts. Venal, hereditary offices therefore now appeared to observers like Diderot a bulwark against despotism, and their disadvantages a price worth paying. Arguments if not from necessity, then at least from public advantage, had come earlier in the century from Montesquieu.[8] He was of course for much of his life the holder of a venal office in the Parlement of Bordeaux (as Voltaire caustically noted) but had left some time before the publication of *De l'esprit des lois* in 1748. Here he argued that in monarchies, whose guiding spirit was honour rather than virtue, the availability of public office for money was an incentive for rich men to aspire to honourable duty, a sort of virtue. He also noted that the only alternative to random recruitment of officials by purchase was appointment by the whims of rulers and their courtiers, since there was no way of objectively identifying merit. Finally he observed that the availability of public offices for sale was an economic incentive to ambitious men to enrich themselves, which was to general advantage. Montesquieu seems in turn to have derived some of these ideas from the *Testament politique* of Cardinal Richelieu, first published in 1688.[9] After half a lifetime at or close to the helm of the state, Richelieu, who had spent his youth denouncing the evils of venality, concluded that it was not without the sort of advantages later listed by Montesquieu. But above all he emphasised the practical problem of how to get rid of it. Too many habits and vested interests would be upset, with unpredictable results, if a 'more austere' regime were to be introduced. Anyway, those who had invested in venal offices would need to be reimbursed. This made abolition quite impractical, however desirable in theory.

In Great Britain, too, acuter minds were prepared to contemplate the uncongenial thought that ostensibly deplorable practices might be necessary. Gibbon, in a celebrated aside, declared that corruption was 'the most infallible symptom of constitutional liberty'.[10] Although not untainted by Gibbon's notorious malicious irony, this opinion was perhaps influenced too by the fact that he sat for a pocket borough in parliament, and enjoyed a sinecure which was among the first to be abolished by the Economical Reformers. Three decades earlier, meanwhile, David Hume had argued at greater length that 'some degree and some kind' of *corruption* and *dependence* (italics his) 'are inseparable from the very nature of the constitution, and necessary to the preservation of our mixed government'.[11]

In the end, however, all these arguments were rationalisations about well established practices. Argument had played little part in the origin and growth either of venality or Old Corruption; any more than it was argument (as I shall contend later) which brought about their downfall. The sale of offices, and parliamentary influence-peddling, had both come about because they enhanced the power and resources of early modern states. They enabled rulers with limited coercive power to tap the liquid assets of their subjects with their consent. Venality flourished through selling hereditary status, authority and professional monopolies. Once lured into investing by these advantages, office-holders could then continue to be deprived of their wealth by manipulating the terms on which they enjoyed them. And not just, or perhaps even primarily, their own wealth: because offices were classed as real property, holders could borrow money on their security, often from lenders who would never dream of offering it directly to the king. Venality additionally brought him a body of servants whom he did not need to pay, except in the form of minimal interest on the initial investment. In England, meanwhile, parliament became essential to kings and queens because it endowed taxation with legitimacy. From the 1690s it also underwrote unprecedented levels of public credit. After the advances in parliament's authority in the sixteenth century, successive monarchs found to their cost that parliament could neither be bypassed nor dispensed with. Means had therefore to be found to control it, and this gave rise to the complex of practices later stigmatised by radicals and reformers. However grotesque in their appearance and consequences, these systems worked. Without venality, Richelieu could not have afforded to enter the Thirty Years' War, and Louis XIV would have come to the end of his resources far sooner. Without the authority and credit of a controlled parliament, the formidable British 'fiscal military state' of the eighteenth century could never have financed its impressive world-wide achievements.[12] It was only when practices admitted to be corrupt, but recognised as effective, ceased to be effective, that their corruptness came to seem significant.

With French venality this began to happen in the military, after the dismal performance of French arms in the Seven Years' War. Military venality had grown up after the collapse of feudalism left rulers obliged to raise armed forces by other means. Lacking the apparatus to do it for themselves, they turned to private colonels and captains, who accordingly retained property in the units they recruited and trained. But by the eighteenth century regiments and companies were being bought for a range of reasons having little enough to do with military efficiency. When in the Seven Years' War a venally-officered French army was humiliated by the more professional Prussians, a reform movement was triggered which culminated in 1776 in a decision to phase out military purchase.[13] No such shock rocked the British military establishment for many more years.[14] Victory over Napoleon by what was now the last venally-officered army in Europe positively reinforced faith in the principle. It was only the disasters of the Crimean War in the 1850s that forced the question of purchase to the forefront of the British military agenda; and when it was finally abolished, in 1871, the time-lag was curiously similar to what it had been in France almost a century earlier. But in both cases a practice long recognised as corrupt only fell when it was shown to impede rather than enhance the efficient pursuit of the state's ends.

Similarly, it was no coincidence that Economical Reform, that attack on the 'wasteful' distribution of royal patronage to buy political support, should have achieved its first triumph in Great Britain in 1782, the moment it became clear that America was lost. Reformers believed that the government which had lost the war had sustained itself, and paid for its misguided and disastrous policies, through 'the influence of the crown', which meant its capacity to corrupt the public life of the country. An even more spectacular example is the fate of the Irish parliament in 1801 – the biggest single attack, perhaps, on the principle we are looking at in British public life over the whole period.[15] Dublin political life was if anything even more permeated by influence-peddling than that of Westminster. The ultimate objective was for Dublin Castle to control Ireland in the British interest. But the Irish rebellion of 1798 showed that these arrangements had failed, and the whole apparatus was abolished in the Act of Union – even if passing it took the most massive deployment of political bribery ever seen in Ireland.

Across the water, meanwhile, Economical Reform was placed on hold by the great war against revolutionary and Napoleonic France: or at least so it appeared to radicals who by this time had coined the term Old Corruption. In fact, Pitt had devoted his first decade in office to the steady elimination of governmental waste; and even though his notorious policy after the outbreak of war was not to mend the roof during a hurricane, the process went on under the rest of his administration and indeed that of his successors.[16] What made it appear to radicals that Old Corruption was as rampant as ever was the undoubted expansion in the state's bureaucratic apparatus and activity over almost a quarter of a century of continuous warfare. Between 1797 and 1815 the number of crown officials employed in England grew by a third.[17] What the radicals did not see was that this was largely the expansion of a salaried bureaucracy which was paid enough to live on, and therefore not expected to make a living from charging the public directly for its services. It was of course costly to the public purse, but this outlay was certainly not now lining the pockets of sinecurists or placemen operating through deputies. And if this new bureaucracy was slimmed down after the war ended, it had nevertheless established itself as the pattern for the future.

The question then is, how could the government afford to give up so many of its powers of patronage or influence? As the Duke of Wellington, then prime minister, observed in 1830, 'I must say that no Government can go on without some means of rewarding services.'[18] In fact he was wrong, and his very presence in office proves it. Because what had brought him to the highest office was less that he was the king's choice, than that he was the leader of a party. This represented a huge change from the days of

Lord North, when party politics were regarded as disreputable. It was scarcely surprising that Edmund Burke, who in *The Present Discontents* of 1770 produced the first reasoned defence of party politics and the legitimacy of opposition, should 12 years later be the instigator of Economical Reform; because the two were quite closely linked. The rise of party provided a means of putting together parliamentary majorities that did not depend on patronage. When governments could depend on the convictions of their followers to deliver them majorities the necessity which had given rise to Old Corruption disappeared.

Nor, perhaps, does this exhaust the longer term implications of the rise of party for this subject. The corollary of party becoming respectable is that opposition became legitimate. By the 1820s it had lost that taint of disloyalty which had clung to it throughout the eighteenth century. By then, the term 'His Majesty's Opposition' was being used with no sense of incongruity. But opposition is an institutionalised public watchdog. Corruption is one of the things it is always on the lookout for, and always ready to denounce. An opposition also knows that, if returned to office, it will be subject to the same scrutiny from the party now out. This is not to say, far from it, that this eliminates corruption in politics. But it does make it harder to sustain, and conceal; and to that extent is bound to diminish its opportunities. Party politics, therefore, not only helped to precipitate the changes we are discussing, but also contributed to their permanence.

One of the most striking arguments offered by Philip Harling in his analysis of the waning of Old Corruption is that the clamour against it was never more loud than when the thing itself was rapidly disappearing.[19] Its radical opponents were kicking against an unlocked door. This was precisely because men in power felt obliged to pre-empt such clamour. In other words, they accepted a certain responsibility to a wider public (even if not, before 1832, to a wider electorate) for the way they spent its taxes. The king's revenues had become the public revenues (though the British now called them 'Crown'), and public men were accordingly the more answerable for their use, or misuse. Ministers had of course been answerable since the seventeenth century to parliament – but when parliament itself was controlled by Old Corruption that did not mean much. By the 1820s, clearly, both ministers *and* parliament felt increasingly answerable to the wider public, and bound to respond to its perceptions. No doubt the presence on the throne of a mad king and his feckless son as regent and then successor had helped to make a mockery of any idea that the state's revenues were the king's; but there were surely deeper forces at work here. The most important was that which drove the wider demand for parliamentary reform between the days of Wilkes and the triumph of reform in the 1830s: the expansion of an educated, well-informed public opinion which demanded a voice in how the country was governed, and resented the greedy oligarchy which had hitherto managed affairs much as it liked, and for the most part in its own narrow interests. Initially this public opinion was relatively easily propitiated. It was satisfied by the fall of North and the first triumphs of Economical Reform under Burke and then Pitt. But by the 1790s satisfying public opinion was less easy. For one thing, the moral earnestness of evangelicalism was increasingly subjecting all corners of public life to searching scrutiny.[20] By these lights, public office was a high calling to be undertaken out of duty rather than for material reward, and one of the obligations incumbent on office-holders or MPs was to set an example to the nation of frugality and self-denial. But even more importantly, by the 1790s the whole landscape of politics had been transformed by the French Revolution.

And so, rather belatedly, we come back to France. There seems little doubt that, directly or indirectly, the French Revolution was by far the most serious and far-reaching precipitant of the changing attitudes we are examining. Research into what brought about this great upheaval is an endless enquiry, which has been particularly intense among scholars since the middle of this century.[21] Amid a myriad of detailed disagreements however, the broadest current consensus is that the Revolution was a symptom of that same emergence of an ever-broader, well educated public opinion, anxious to play its part in public affairs, that I have just been discussing in the British context. Despite a censorship of the press and the book trade that had no parallel across the Channel, there were few aspects of public affairs that were not intensively discussed in late eighteenth-century France. What was common to all these discussions was the assumption that there was no real chance of doing anything about even the most glaring abuses or anomalies, including venality.[22] The Revolution showed that this assumption was wrong.

Although it is possible for historians to offer coherent explanations of how and why it came about, it is clear that contemporaries did not expect or predict it. But when, to everyone's surprise, the French monarchy, and the fabric of authority that sustained it, collapsed in the summer of 1788, suddenly *anything* became possible, no issue was off the agenda, and what had seemed like Utopian dreams became potentially realisable. And however much of what was attempted in France in and after 1789 went horribly wrong, and produced results that nobody had intended, after the Revolution happened the lesson remained. Nothing was beyond reform, or at least beyond the attempt. Nothing was so fixed in the nature of things that it could not be challenged, and perhaps overthrown. This thought certainly concentrated the minds of British public men as they made Herculean efforts to fight revolutionary and Napoleonic France on the one hand, and sought to fend off public allegations of their own corruption on the other. The spectre of the French Revolution haunted every stage in the later waning of British Old Corruption.

The essential first step of the Revolution had, in fact, achieved at one blow what we saw earlier took several generations in Great Britain. On 17 June 1789 the Third Estate deputies proclaimed themselves the National Assembly and cancelled and then re-authorised all taxes in the name of the French Nation. With that act the Nation (or representatives in its name) seized sovereignty from the king. The struggles of the next month, culminating in the fall of the Bastille, guaranteed the triumph of this transfer of authority and legitimacy. It meant that henceforth the revenues handled by and emoluments paid to officials were national not royal business; and subject to legitimate public censure if misused or misappropriated. Public accountability was established; and even when, later, Napoleon largely abandoned representative institutions, he proved a bureaucratic ruler who subjected his officials to the supervision of a public Court of Accounts. He, like the community of taxpayers represented in assemblies before and after him, had every interest in the public revenues being spent honestly and efficiently. When the Restoration brought a return of parliamentary government, the granting and supervision of the state's revenues was made one of the main concerns of a Chamber of Deputies which for a variety of reasons was never disposed to give free rein to the executive. And since parliamentary government was new in France, nothing like Old Corruption as a system of managing parliamentary power had developed, or stood in need of abolition. This, indeed, was the one aspect of British practice that no French regime was ever moved to admire, or imitate.

Nevertheless there had once been a French equivalent. The men of 1789 were determined to abolish a complex of behaviour and practice – privilege, monopolies, nepotism and patrimoniality – that was not unlike Old Corruption across the Channel. It was not held together by the requirements of parliamentary management, but it was just as all-pervasive in the way public affairs were run in France. It was what was attacked when, in the Declaration of the Rights of Man and the Citizen of 26 August 1789, the destined preamble to the constitution they aimed to give France, the men of 1789 proclaimed equality before the law and careers open to talent and merit. One clear implication of this was that it would no longer be permissible to recruit to public service by venality. When in the spring of 1789, at the time of elections to the Estates-General, all electors were invited, in what might be called the first public opinion poll of modern times, to declare what they wanted their assembled representatives to do, hardly any of the *cahiers* in which they did so defended the sale of offices. Even the only newish argument in its favour, the argument that Diderot had found so persuasive in 1771, that venal tenure was an obstacle to despotism, lost its force when the country was to be governed by a representative assembly rather than an absolute monarch. What the *cahiers* were full of was traditional arguments against venality: that it was wrong to buy and sell offices which gave men power and authority over their fellow citizens without any guarantee of competence; wrong to be able to dispose of public offices privately or by heredity; wrong to be able to charge fees for public services that ought to be free; wrong to grant public monopolies in return for payment.[23] In a strict sense none of these practices were corrupt, because all were perfectly legal and open. For the authors of the *cahiers*, however, corruption lay in the very law which permitted such things.

This, as I noted earlier, had always been the conviction of the vast majority of Frenchmen who had ever spoken or written about venality in general terms.[24] Even the defenders cited earlier were reluctant ones. Parallels can also be found for the religiously-motivated disapproval of Old Corruption by evangelicals.

The young Richelieu had denounced the sale of offices when he was a spokesman for the clergy in 1614; and the boost given to all aspects of venality by the financial needs of Louis XIV's last two years was condemned on moral grounds by Protestants like Jurieu, devout Catholics like Fénelon, and widely-read Jansenists like Duguet. At the other end of the intellectual spectrum, the later Voltaire was a persistent critic of what he regarded as a shameful abuse.[25] The *cahiers* of 1789 demonstrated how widely shared this perception was. Those who drew them up authorised their representatives to attack the practice root and branch; and that is what they proceeded to do, beginning with the ringing abolition of venality on 4 August of that very same year.

In the event, the whole process took over five years and was riddled with all sorts of complexities.[26] Even so, it was a far cry from the 90-year process in Great Britain running from Burke's Economical Reforms to the final abolition of military purchase. What facilitated the relatively rapid winding up of the whole system in France was that the revolutionaries found a way of paying off the 70,000 or so holders of venal offices. This had always been seen as the most insuperable obstacle to eliminating venality. Nobody ever seriously thought that it could be abolished without compensating those who had invested in offices, and the cost of that was always regarded as prohibitive. It took a revolution to think the unthinkable, and actually translate the thought into reality. Even then the burden on the finances was so colossal that periodically a suspension of the process was proposed. Nor were most office-holders satisfied with the end result, since the compensation they received was substantially less than their offices had been worth on the market. Nevertheless by 1794 it had been largely accomplished, and an institution condemned from the start as corrupt, but which had grown and flourished, seemingly unstoppably, over five centuries, had been bought out. Contrast

Great Britain, where a far less extensive apparatus could only be dismantled piecemeal, and where compensation, though agreed to be just, was only paid out with extreme reluctance.[27] The Irish Act of Union, indeed, for all its urgency, only got through the parliament in Dublin at the second attempt, after substantial compensation was promised to borough owners who were to be dispossessed.[28]

Something else was promised too, on that occasion, if only tacitly: peerages, or promotions in the peerage for those who voted the right way, or ensured that those whose votes they controlled did so.[29] This, too, was one of the hallowed practices of Old Corruption, but it also pointed the way to a less corrupt political world. For peerages cost nothing. They were not offices carrying emoluments, but distinctions of honour; rewards for past services, rather than advance payment on future ones. The massive expansion in the numbers in the House of Lords over this period[30] seems actually to be a corollary of the retreat of Old Corruption. When men could win the rewards and recognition they wanted with honours, there was no need to buy them with more material inducements. This is the argument still often heard today in Britain in defence of the so-called 'Honours System', the twice yearly distribution of titles and medals that fills two close-printed pages of all the serious newspapers: it is a harmless preventative against corruption. Whether it *is* harmless, or whether it does prevent corruption, are different questions: in the 1920s Lloyd-George notoriously sold peerages to swell Liberal Party funds, and there have been occasional allegations of the same order since. Nevertheless the point stands, and it is the same one made by Napoleon in defence of the Legion of Honour which he introduced. They may be baubles, but it is by baubles that men are governed. It is probably no coincidence that his particular bauble is still much worn and coveted in the France of the Fifth Republic.

In other words, if practices deemed to be corrupt are to be
openly recognised as such, and prohibited or abandoned when the
necessities which sustained them disappear or are shown no longer
to be necessary, there will probably remain functions which they
fulfilled which need to be provided for by other means. Conferring
honours and distinctions is one such function. Even more
important is the provision of services and a personnel delivering
them, by more publicly acceptable means. That means first of all
a properly salaried bureaucracy. If those in power or authority,
at whatever level, are not paid enough, it is inevitable that they
will seek remuneration outside or beyond their duties. Uncorrupt
bureaucracies do not come cheap, as the Prussian state which had
pioneered such an institution, and later provided Max Weber with
his paradigms,[31] recognised. The French and the British, as they
struggled out of venality and Old Corruption, learned that lesson
the hard way. British radicals who argued that MPs should be paid
so that they did not need either private means, or patronage which
made them dependent, were at the same time very reluctant to
see public funds spent on adequate salaries for civil servants, or
adequate numbers of them, for fear that taxpayers' money would
be squandered as before by sinecurists.[32]

Secondly there was the question of recruitment. French
defenders of venality like Richelieu or Montesquieu argued that if
offices had to be bought at least they would not be filled through
nepotism, clientage, or favouritism – in other words the whims
of the powerful. They could envisage no way of independently
identifying merit or capacity. But the French revolutionaries, and
the drafters of the *cahiers* which initially legitimised their reforming
impulses, believed there was a way. They thought all public officials
should be elected, as if the perceptions of one's fellow citizens
were enough to identify merit. The flaws in such a conviction are
obvious, but they scarcely had time to emerge before the country

relapsed into authoritarianism. When it re-emerged after 1814, election only survived for legislators. Under Napoleon, meanwhile, a start had been made on recruiting officials on the basis of certain minimal qualifications, or of passing certain examinations.[33] This was the true pattern of the future, and it was soon beginning to be adopted in Great Britain too.[34] By the 1850s, recruitment by open competitive examination was being recommended (though not yet generally accepted) for the entire civil service. Similar trends were observable under the July Monarchy in France.[35] In other words, over the early nineteenth century objective criteria and workable procedures were slowly elaborated for identifying merit and capacity in the recruitment and promotion of public officials. The numbers applying for selection under these procedures also shows that educational systems were producing no shortage of well qualified candidates. In these circumstances there was decreasing room for patronage, patrimoniality, nepotism, venality – all practices which it was now increasingly acceptable to stigmatise openly as aspects of public corruption.

Whether this diminished the influence of the wealthy in public life is a different question. Philip Harling argues that the repudiation of Old Corruption actually helped to consolidate and perpetuate the power of Britain's wealthy ruling elite.[36] No wonder Aristotle remained required reading at the schools and universities where they were educated.

PART II

THE OLD ORDER DISINTEGRATES

CHAPTER 5

The Union with Ireland in a European Context

For anyone so improbable as a historian of France to presume to discuss a landmark of British and Irish history requires some explanation. It lies in a bizarre twist of professional history which left me, for the best part of 20 years, teaching late eighteenth-century Ireland as a special subject. My research interest however, always lay in the ancien régime in France.

One of the most striking, fundamental, and – to my mind – exhilarating characteristics of that old order is its sheer institutional variety, that baffling chaos which later revolutionaries tried to replace with something simpler, more rational, and more uniform. My initial subject of research was the Parlement of Bordeaux, one of those 'sovereign' courts of law which exercised final appellate jurisdiction over part of the king's realms, and enjoyed certain legislative powers there, too, including the right to criticise proposed new laws. The jurisdictional area of this parlement was extensive: scarcely smaller, perhaps than Ireland. But there were others as big, or bigger, and a number a good deal smaller too. Roughly, it corresponded to the old duchy of Aquitaine, that Plantagenet fief finally reconquered from English rule in the mid-fifteenth century. Those of other provincial parlements corresponded similarly to other formerly independent or semi-independent counties, duchies and even kingdoms (in the case of Navarre) accruing over the centuries to the king of France. And in a number of these there was a further complication not present at Bordeaux. Parlements like those of Languedoc, Brittany or Burgundy shared, or vied for, authority with estates. In these provinces there were representative bodies with powers to grant taxes and loans to the monarch, and to administer various public works.[1] Posterity conventionally thinks of pre-revolutionary France as an absolute monarchy, where rulers did not share their power. Kings habitually claimed as much, and those who later overthrew them found self-justification in accepting their claims, if only for the purpose of triumphant repudiation. But in practice, for both sides, this was more a matter of assertion than objective description. The reality of the ancien régime was intense confusion of powers and perpetual overlaps of unequal jurisdiction, in which the king, so far from imposing an unchallengeable authority, was constantly bargaining with his subjects at a number of different levels. And one way of bargaining with subjects, especially new ones, was to grant or confirm on an ad hoc basis the very powers which were later seen to impede royal authority. The parlements of most provinces, or their estates, owed their new or continued existence to 'capitulations' or confirmations at the moment when the king of France became their ruler. Nor were these concessions invariably shrouded in the mists of the middle ages. When Lorraine finally fell to Louis XV in 1766, a parlement was almost automatically established at Nancy. Later still, newly annexed Corsica was endowed with a sovereign court (1768) and with estates (1770).

The results were chaotic, inconsistent, and self-contradictory, but this was the institutional ancien régime, and for several centuries it worked. Nor (although the term ancien régime was invented by the French revolutionaries who destroyed it) was this pattern exclusively French. Early modern Europe was largely made up of what have been called composite monarchies,[2] built up, and sometimes in turn split up, by a complex process of dynasticism or conquest. When territories changed rulers, they seldom changed institutions. Only denial of a new ruler's legitimacy through physical resistance was likely to result on his part in denial of his new subjects' claims to distinctive treatment and particular privilege, as when Philip V of Spain cancelled the *fueros* of the crown of Aragon in 1707.[3] But this was rare. In a Europe where dynastic right was generally acknowledged to be the best entitlement to authority, few subjects felt justified in rejecting the ruler whom God had given them, however apparently random His methods. When they did so, as in the case of the Dutch rebels against Philip II, or indeed the inhabitants of these islands twice in the seventeenth century, it was because religious differences made it less than clear what God had actually intended. But that vast majority who never did contest a change of ruler usually found themselves rewarded by respect for their institutions, including representative ones. At the level of provinces, or sub-kingdoms in composite monarchies, representative bodies were more widespread than is often recognised among observers dazzled by the apparent progress of 'absolutism'. What they overlook is a complex and infinitely diverse set of public practices, a continent-wide institutional ancien régime, or what a late-seventeenth-century writer described as Europe's 'noble gothic constitution'.[4]

Two hundred years ago, a century after the writer's death, the phrase would have struck instant chords in Belfast. For he was of course William Molyneux, whose *Case of Ireland* of 1698 was one of the sacred texts of Irish legislative independence.[5] Every educated Irishman would have heard of an author invoked by Henry Grattan in his famous speech celebrating the achievement of legislative independence in 1782. Molyneux's argument (at this point in his text at least) was that Ireland's separate legislature, with its independent powers under the crown, was an example of a 'universal' pattern in Europe of parliamentary government, a pattern which he thought should be preserved '*Sacred and Inviolable*' wherever it was found. Ireland, then – although Molyneux could not have conceived of a term invented only 90 years after his death – was a typical enough specimen of a Europe-wide ancien régime.

Over the past few years there has been extensive discussion of the idea launched by Jonathan Clark that there was an English ancien régime which came to an end between 1828 and 1832.[6] But it was largely about England alone that Clark advanced the idea, and the key to his conception of an ancien régime state was that it was 'confessional', the central characteristic being a politico-religious exclusivism. This was certainly typical enough of eighteenth-century European states; but it should be remembered that by then England was no longer a state in itself. It was part of a wider composite monarchy under the British crown; and this made it not less but even more typically an ancien régime entity. In statutory legal terms from 1707 England did not exist at all, although Englishmen, as they always have, tended to use the word to include everybody else on the island of Great Britain. Technically, after the Act of Union, the former England was merely South Britain.[7] And North Britain, if it gave up its separate parliament for a share of the representation at Westminster, retained its own legal system, a distinct religious establishment, and a whole host of other peculiar institutions which had remained unaltered, just as England's had, when dynastic fate brought the two crowns onto a single head in 1603. It is true that Scotland's distinct institutions survived as the result of a treaty between jurisdictionally equal partners, whereas under a continental monarch they would have figured as a confirmation of privileges. They remained privileges all the same, in the sense of an entitlement to special, separate treatment that conferred advantages.

The material value of those advantages for Scotland became obvious soon enough, and it was foreseen from the start by Irish observers. Molyneux was dead by the time the crisis broke which precipitated the Act of Union of 1707; but in a passage dropped from the 1782 edition of the *Case of Ireland*, he spoke wistfully of a legislative union with England as the best of all solutions for Ireland, but one which was 'an happiness we can hardly hope for'.[8] As it became clear under Queen Anne that a union between England and Scotland was likely to happen, the Irish parliament itself began to petition for inclusion in it, and went on doing so for some time after the Scottish union became a reality.[9] But Scotland had blackmailed England in a way that Protestant Ireland as represented in the Dublin parliament never could, by threatening to restore the Stuarts. It was only when, almost a century later, an even more alarming threat of independence came from across the water that the rulers of Great Britain were prepared to contemplate a widening of the union to include Ireland.

And meanwhile the Irish parliament carried on, a legislative body representing a substantial part of the king's dominions, the separate realm of Ireland. Was it so different, in the British composite monarchy, from, say, the Hungarian Diet under the Habsburgs, or the parliament of Sicily under the Neapolitan Bourbons, or the estates of Cleves and Mark under the Hohenzollerns, or the estates of French *pays d'états* like Languedoc or Brittany? It was often enough compared, in the 1760s and 1770s, and many a time since by historians right down to Roy Foster, to the colonial legislatures of North America.[10] But unlike them it was practically coeval in age with the English parliament, and by Molyneux's day there was an extensive mythology, upon which he liberally drew, about its origins and early powers and development.[11] Similar cherished myths shrouded the origins of other European legislatures. In Poland and Hungary, they traced the freedom which they claimed to symbolise to conquerors, Sarmatians or Magyars, who by virtue of their conquests enjoyed a monopoly of representation and alone had the right to speak for all the inhabitants of their territories.[12] Molyneux explicitly invoked the Polish comparison, perhaps more appositely than he consciously intended, for throughout most of its history down to 1793 the Irish parliament, too, was happy to represent only a minority which owed its power to conquest, English-speaking exclusively from the start, and Protestant exclusively for all but the briefest periods throughout the seventeenth and eighteenth centuries. In real, though not strictly jurisdictional terms, the Polish comparison could be pushed even further, since for most of the eighteenth century the Polish-Lithuanian Commonwealth was in effect a Russian substate, and the real ruler not the elected monarch, but the Russian ambassador. In Polish historiography the period from 1773 to 1788 is known as the proconsulate – a term not far removed from viceroyalty.[13]

There are other contemporary parallels. It has often been pointed out, for example, that there was little that modern eyes would regard as representative in the way members of so-called representative bodies were chosen under the ancien régime.[14] Where elections took place, as in Poland or Sweden, they were seldom open contests, and were dominated by magnate influence. Would it be fair to say anything else of Ireland? Notoriously, no general election at all took place between 1727 and 1761. Many Irish seats were in effect the private property of noble patrons, and all members of the upper house sat, like many members of continental estates, by right of office. None of this was identical to any other legislature, even Westminster. If Dublin undeniably mirrored Westminster, the mirror was a distorting one. But the whole essence of the institutional ancien régime was that nothing *was* quite like anything else. Everything was, in a legal sense, particular and peculiar, and the Irish parliament did not differ more from, say, the estates of Brittany than they in turn differed from the assembly of communities of Provence. Some French provincial estates sat annually, others biennially just like the Irish parliament. They had intermediary commissions to see that their business got done when they were not sitting, which it is surely not altogether fanciful to compare to the Lords Justices who administered Ireland between parliaments before the viceroyalty of Townshend. In France, as in Ireland, the sitting of a provincial legislature required the presence of the king's representative, the governor, who would open the proceedings in the sovereign's name. One of his duties was to see that business was smoothly managed, and he needed reliable managers for that – what in Ireland were called undertakers. These systems seldom malfunctioned in France. And in Ireland, until Townshend's attack on the undertakers after 1768, there were only two serious parliamentary crises in the eighteenth century – Wood's Halfpence in the 1720s and the Money Bill furore in the 1750s. It was a record a good deal less turbulent than that of the estates of Brittany, for instance, or the Hungarian Diet.

In point of powers, continental parallels were even closer. The prime function of all these representative institutions was to authorise taxation by giving a semblance of consent from those who had to pay it. By the eighteenth century (appearances in the Money Bill crisis to the contrary) the days of refusing supply were long gone. The king's ministers decided what they needed, and secured it by a process of back room bargaining with the local power-brokers before any formal proposal reached the floor. And who were those power-brokers? Office-holders and prelates, who were rewarded for their co-operation with patronage. These words, apart from the irresistible reference to the Money Bill, have been carefully chosen; they could apply equally well to the parliament of Ireland, or to the estates of Languedoc. Both raised their revenue from a specific pattern of fiscality, quite distinct from that falling on most of the king's other subjects: in Ireland there was no land tax; in Languedoc the *taille*, the basic direct tax, fell on land rather than on persons. Both legislatures made themselves responsible for an extensive range of public works, such as roads and canals. Both took a special interest in excluding religious dissidents from and power or influence within their jurisdiction, for, in both, religious civil war was something within living memory.[15] What neither did, and no comparable body elsewhere tried to do either, was to challenge the king's right to make general policy for all his dominions. In Ireland Poynings' Law made sure of that, reinforced from 1720 by the Sixth of George I – even if most of the English statutes applicable to Ireland between then and 1782 were quite uncontentious.[16] The occasion for that notorious Act had actually been jurisdictional rather than legislative, to establish the overriding appellate authority of the British House of Lords over all the king's dominions. The French comparison here is more aptly with the parlements, whose 'sovereign' authority was theoretically final in their areas but who found themselves struggling constantly against the 'evocation' of sensitive cases to the Privy Council.[17]

In yet another area of the Irish parliament's competence, there is an obvious comparison with the estates of the Habsburg hereditary dominions. This was in raising troops, and paying for their upkeep. The crisis of the European ancien régime, out of which the age of revolution was born, began when states of military ambition sought to expand their capacities and find new ways of paying for it. The first power to confront this problem was the House of Habsburg, which in the aftermath of the loss of Silesia in the Austrian Succession War sought to upgrade and expand its armed forces by removing their financing and recruitment from the control of the various provincial estates. It dressed this up as a boon to them, demanding in return a ten-year 'recess' in which the estates surrendered their freedom to grant taxes. Those contesting this dubious bargain had it forced upon them by an assumed 'royal right'.[18] The British state in its turn felt the need for enhanced military readiness, this time to defend its gains from the Seven Years' War. This was the purpose of George Grenville's ill-fated Stamp Tax of 1763, which inaugurated the movement towards American independence. It was also the brief given to Townshend when he became Lord-Lieutenant of Ireland in 1767. He was instructed to carry an increase of troops on the Irish establishment from 12,000 to 15,000; and he forced it through, if not by some royal right, at least by a ruthless resumption of royal patronage that rewrote the ground rules of Irish parliamentary politics and paved the way for the struggles of 1778–82.[19]

With those struggles we enter the age of revolution proper, which culminated for Ireland in the loss of the representative institutions which so far this chapter has been attempting to set in a structural context. What now about the developments which brought the Irish parliament to such a momentous end in 1800–1? Were they *sui generis* or can they be seen as part of wider processes affecting ancien régime states in general? The most immediately striking aspect of the history of the Irish parliament between 1767 and 1801 is surely the way that its extinction followed a quarter of a century in which its power and independence had seemingly grown. There are certain parallels for this. Poland again offers one of the most obvious. In 1788, with the Russian power distracted by a Turkish war, the Polish legislature, the *seym*, began a four-year session in which Russian tutelage was thrown off, and a new constitution adopted on 3 May 1791 designed to secure Polish autonomy.[20] All this built on a generation of vigorous national consciousness-raising since the partition of 1772.[21] In Ireland the so-called constitution of 6 April 1782 was equally the culmination of a generation of patriotic rhetoric at a time when the dominant power was weakened and distracted by foreign war.

What happened in Poland was all too dangerous in a Europe threatened by the French Revolution. Attempts to curb it by the surrounding powers, indeed, led to a national rebellion in 1794 which acknowledged the inspiration of the French Revolution and vainly appealed to Paris for help.[22] It was put down, largely by the Russians, with appalling slaughter, and in the aftermath the *seym* was compelled to vote itself out of existence and Poland disappeared as a distinct entity from the map of Europe. The Commonwealth's separate existence, and its peculiar institutions, had simply become more trouble than they were worth. An independent Poland, controlled in fact from St. Petersburg but handling its own internal affairs, through the representative institution of its social elite, had seemed since the days of Peter the Great the best way to ensure the stability of eastern Europe. By the 1790s, however, it was repeatedly endangering that stability, and flirting too with a movement – the French Revolution – which challenged the legitimacy of all established authorities. A lot of this ought to sound familiar. As in the comparison made earlier with Languedoc, only a word or two needs to be changed to make this a description of what happened in Ireland. Authority devolved to a local aristocracy, and its representative assembly, eventually provoked more trouble than it had first been tolerated in order to dispel. In both cases the struggle against the French Revolution exacerbated matters. Eventually the threatened power felt only safe in absorbing these troubled dependencies into a system of more direct control.

In both cases, too, there was an outcry; because this absorption ran against what those who witnessed or experienced it had been educated to expect. The effect of the age of revolution, for all its rhetoric, was to destroy representative institutions wholesale, not consolidate them – but the expectations out of which it developed were quite the opposite. The roots of late-eighteenth-century revolutions can be found in mid-century 'patriotism' – the sentiment that a country was being ill-served by its existing, established form of government (or at least those who were running it) and that the solution lay in making institutions more representative of those with the true interests of the country at heart. There was nothing unique about the Irish self-styled patriots who opposed undertaker or castle influence in parliament, demanded an Irish habeas corpus and Militia Bill, sought regular general elections, and denounced Poynings' Law or the Sixth of George I. When the Americans rebelled, Irish patriots saw instant parallels between colonists protesting at being taxed without representation under the British crown, and their own subordinate situation. But there were plenty of continental parallels, too. In addition to the Poles, there were Dutch patriots who denounced oligarchy and the ambitions of the Prince of Orange,[23] Belgian patriots who resisted the rationalising despotism of Joseph II,[24] Hungarian patriots outraged by the same monarch's refusal to acknowledge their peculiar institutions and privileges,[25] or French opponents of Louis XV's attempts to remodel and silence the parlements, who called themselves patriots 18 years before the term became synonymous in France with revolutionary.[26] Nor were Irish patriots unique in their readiness to take up arms in furtherance of their convictions. The Volunteers had counterparts in the Dutch Free Corps, the Belgian *Pro Aris et Focis* militias (this motto was adopted by some Volunteer companies),[27] and most spectacularly in the French National Guard of 1789.

The Irish patriots believed, perhaps justifiably, that their activity, once they became an armed mass movement among Protestants, had brought about British agreement first to 'free trade', then to the repeal of Poynings' Law and the Sixth of George I, which made Ireland a notionally equal partner to Great Britain under the crown of George III. But was what made Pitt (whose ministry was almost co-terminous with Grattan's parliament) prepared to tolerate Irish legislative independence perhaps a genuine receptivity to the potential of devolved representation?[28] If he was indeed open to such possibilities, he was certainly not alone in Europe. Necker, the ministerial miracle-worker who had paid for French involvement in the American War of Independence without new direct taxes, was a professed believer in the representation of taxpayers in the processes of government. In 1778 he had introduced two provincial assemblies in areas hitherto without estates and was projecting a third when he fell from power in 1781. He was proud of their achievements, and did not cease to trumpet them through his well-oiled publicity machine in subsequent years.[29] In 1787 Calonne, whose reform plan precipitated the pre-revolutionary crisis, proposed the generalisation of such provincial assemblies. Several of them actually sat and began work under his successor Brienne.[30] But from the start it was feared that such assemblies, which, despite their names, did not sit in historic provinces but in generalities (the administrative districts of the agents of absolute monarchy, the intendants), would be bodies of stooges, with neither the power nor the courage to resist the demands of authority. Since mid-century, in fact, there had been growing support for an alternative representative model – the generalisation of provincial estates. Some parlements in provinces which had lost them had begun to call for their restoration from the 1750s onwards, and others joined them once Louis XVI was on the throne.[31] These demands were reinforced when Corsica was given new estates and existing ones such as those of Languedoc or Brittany managed to increase their powers in various ways over the same years.[32] The pre-revolutionary crisis brought the movement to a head when Brienne capitulated to the demands of two provinces to be represented by estates rather than by his projected assemblies. Provence was allowed the full form of its old

estates, last assembled in 1639. Dauphiné was granted the first
assembly of any kind since 1628. And once these concessions were
made, the movement snowballed, and every province was soon
clamouring for its own estates, whether or not they had enjoyed
them historically. Not only that. Many of them based their claims
in the rhetoric of distinct national identity. The Dauphinois,
whose example did most to inspire this movement, started calling
themselves the Dauphinois 'nation'; it came as no problem to the
Bretons to call themselves a nation, and soon less probable areas
were claiming nationhood. The first important thing ever written
by Robespierre, which doubtless he was happy enough soon to
forget, was a pamphlet addressed *À la Nation artésienne*, about the
form to be taken by restored estates in Artois.[33]

In the event, all this came to nothing. Once Louis XVI conceded
that the Estates-General, themselves defunct since 1614, would
meet in 1789, attention throughout his realms became concentrated
on them, and the form they should take. Although there was a
widespread conviction, especially among the nobility, that the
deputies to the Estates-General should be chosen by provincial
estates, that was only allowed to happen in the case of Dauphiné,
Béarn and Navarre. The decision of December 1788 to opt for
other methods stopped the movement for revived provincial estates
dead in its tracks; and despite considerable continued support for
them in the *cahiers* of the following spring, it was an idea that
the National Assembly showed no interest in when it embarked
later in 1789 on its reform of French administration. It is true
that the constitution of 1791 enshrined a considerable measure of
devolution, but it was of a standard, uniform sort which took no
account of historic provinces and their privileges. In any case, it
did not last. The 'Jacobin' pattern of representation bequeathed to
France by the Revolution was to be posited on a nation 'one and
indivisible', whose only legitimate representatives sat in a single

national legislature, directly elected. It is a pattern that has only begun to be diluted under the regional devolution set in train since the 1960s by the Fifth Republic.

It was to such a Jacobin regime that the desperate Polish patriots appealed for help in 1794, seeing in its aspirations a parallel to their own doomed constitution of 3 May 1791. The heirs to the Dutch patriots, whose hopes had been snuffed out by Prussian invasion in 1787, also worked after their emancipation by the French in 1795 to give the new Batavian Republic a French style unitary representative constitution quite distinct from that of the old loosely federal United Provinces. And that was certainly the aspiration of the United Irishmen after 1795 – help from the French to establish in Ireland an independent legislature for a republic one and certainly indivisible. What they most emphatically did not want, having begun themselves in 1791 as a movement for parliamentary reform, was the Irish parliament – as constituted at any time in its history, remote or recent. However much they failed to achieve, they were certainly instrumental in securing this end, at least.

The precise way in which the Irish parliament met its end, and the local implications for the conduct of British and Irish public life, are beyond the scope of this chapter.[34] The purpose here is to try to see the Union from a much greater distance, and in a much wider setting. The key must lie in the French Revolution. Part of its origin lay in a desire for greater representation in government through devolution, that same desire which fuelled Irish demands for greater autonomy under the British crown. And if this aspect of the Revolution's origin is now largely forgotten, it is because for a complex set of reasons the settlement which emerged was committed to a single, centralised form of representation. That commitment entailed the abandonment of the rich and varied luxuriance of ancien régime institutions, including parlements and provincial estates. They were now seen as more likely to impede than to promote the legitimate activity of government. The behaviour of the Irish parliament, both before and after 1782, confronted George III's ministers with the same conundrum. Even as they made concession to patriot demands on free trade or legislative independence, both Lord North and Shelburne's Whigs pondered whether Ireland might not be more easily governable under 'an union'.[35] Pitt was more agnostic. He thought legislative independence could be made to work, given the right reforms,[36] but what finally made such reforms impossible, again, was the revolution in France, in the manifold ways in which it impacted upon the Irish body politic.

Above all, the Revolution helped to revive the Catholic question. The one area for comparison with the continent scarcely touched upon so far is the religious one, and this is because there was no true continental parallel to a legislative assembly which only represented a religious minority. Even in Languedoc, where sectarian antagonism was as strong as in Ireland, the oppressed Protestants were only in a majority in a few districts. Even so, what the French revolutionaries did to give Protestants civil and political equality[37] was instrumental in reviving the question of Catholic equality in Ireland; both by highlighting the intrinsic injustice of anything else, and by showing that Catholics in power were not natural oppressors.[38] And then, when the new regime in France began to quarrel with the Catholic Church, the prospect opened up in the British body politic, for the first time since the Reformation,[39] that Catholicism under the British crown might be turned into a fund of loyalty rather than potential treason. Accordingly, the years between 1791 and 1793 became, as it were, a race between the United Irishmen and the British government to capture the support of the Catholics of Ireland. The Dublin parliament found itself sidelined, even though it would have to bear any immediate consequences. It was now that the term *Ascendancy* was first coined – rather like the term ancien régime in France – to describe an order assumed to be on the verge of extinction.[40]

Yet the encounter with the French Revolution was to produce a further twist. When the French invasion of the Austrian Netherlands pitched Great Britain into war, reform of any sort was put on hold. This gave the Irish parliament a last chance to prove its value in what had always been its primary function from the perspective of London, which was to keep Ireland under control in the British interest. It failed. Within five years its ineffectual intransigence had helped to provoke a rebellion, largely among the very Catholics whom Pitt had hoped to turn into a bulwark of resistance to the menace from France. Instead, driven to desperation by the savage though supposedly pre-emptive tactics of the Ascendancy's executive, Catholics positively begged the French to intervene as their ancestors had a century earlier. And, even though the French response was poor compared with that sent by Louis XIV to support James II, the Ascendancy could not cope with it. It had to be rescued from General Humbert and his peasant auxiliaries by money and troops from across the water. The Dublin parliament, meanwhile, now boycotted even by the very Whigs and patriots who had previously trumpeted its independent pretensions, had lost all relevance to what was happening in Ireland.

And so the French revolutionaries, who destroyed the institutional ancien régime first in their own country, and then wherever else they went, were also instrumental in destroying it even where they did *not* go – or at least not in significant numbers. In his classic analysis of *The Ancien Régime and the Revolution*, Tocqueville argued that the historic mission of the French Revolution was to destroy the remaining obstacles to the power of the centralised state. More recently this perception has been reformulated into the proposition that the Revolution liberated not so much the people as the state.[41] But once that had been done in France, and the energies thus released channelled into war against all major powers of Europe, sooner or later those powers, if they were to survive, had to liberate themselves in the same way from the shackles of their own ancien régime structures. Napoleon, the Revolution's heir, was defeated in the end not by the ancien régime – which he completed the Revolution's work by destroying outside France as well as within – but by states reformed and remodelled along parallel lines. The great exception to this generalisation is supposed to have been Great Britain, secure and untouched beyond its natural moat. From an anglocentric perspective I suppose that is just about sustainable – although even here the extent of administrative reform during those supposedly frozen years has often been underestimated.[42] And this is to overlook the elimination of the most glaring of ancien régime aspects of the British state, the separate sub-kingdom of Ireland and its distinct legislature, Britain's Achilles heel in its life-or-death struggle with the sworn enemy of all ancien régime institutions. Whether that elimination strengthened the British body politic for any other purpose than the defeat of France is, of course, a very different question.

The French Revolution: Possible because Thinkable or Thinkable because Possible?

Over the last 30 or so years, the writings of Keith Baker have played a pivotal part in our developing understanding of the French Revolution and how it came about. He has taught us to rethink the entire problem of the intellectual and ideological origins of the Revolution, and has been a major orchestrator of collective efforts by his colleagues to explore this field. In a justly famous article of 1982,[1] he laid emphasis on what he called the 'intellectual stock' of a society in determining how it sees itself and what it is doing. He has certainly brought his own contribution to the intellectual stock of the field in which he works. Intellectual stock, he argues, is made up of 'bits and pieces' that 'come in handy'; and it is on one of these bits and pieces thrown up by his work that I want to focus.

In another article[2] published five years later, he laid emphasis on the forum in which pre-revolutionary French society deployed its intellectual stock: the sphere of public opinion. 'Public opinion', he concluded, 'had become the articulating concept of a new political space with a legitimacy and authority apart from that of the crown: a public space in which the nation could reclaim its rights against the crown. Within this space, the French Revolution became thinkable.'

This proved an idea with a future, as I hope a few brief examples will demonstrate. Roger Chartier defined his investigation of the cultural origins of the French Revolution in 1990 as an attempt 'to spot certain of the conditions which made it possible, possible because thinkable'.[3] Another example is David Bell, who in his book on the *Cult of the Nation* tells us that the cult of great men 'contributed deeply to the cultural shifts which made Revolutionary radicalism thinkable'.[4] From Daniel Gordon comes a somewhat less explicit formulation, which nevertheless seems to be saying much the same thing. 'Only the elaboration of an alternative vision of political order could have brought about political change.'[5]

We could go on adding examples, but the introduction of these influential figures ought to be enough to show that this is an approach to the French Revolution now widely accepted among those who currently define the field. What it appears to postulate is two things. One is that the outlook of the revolutionaries was formed before the Revolution began, under the old regime. The other is that things do not happen unless we are mentally prepared for them. It seems to me that the first of these propositions needs, at the very least, to be carefully glossed; and that the second needs to be more-or-less frontally challenged.

In one sense it is obvious that the outlook of the revolutionaries was formed before the Revolution occurred. Nobody who played any significant role in it was born much after 1770, and by 1789 the education of even the youngest of them was largely over. Whatever occurred in or after that year was in interaction with minds formed and stocked beforehand, in pre-revolutionary ways. There is still important research to be done on that formation, which for many occurred amid the educational and experimental chaos which followed the expulsion of the Jesuits. The point to make now, however, is this. To say that the minds of the revolutionaries were formed before 1789 is not necessarily to say, in the celebrated words of John Adams about another revolution, that the revolution was in the minds of the people in the course of 15 years before a drop of blood was shed. Nobody foresaw or foretold what would happen in the decade beginning in 1789: that was precisely why so many people found it shocking, appalling, and – dare we say it? – unthinkable. It is relatively easy to unearth voices, and famous ones, during the preceding half century, predicting that some sort of revolution was bound to occur in France. But this does not necessarily tell us that they foresaw the one that did occur; much less that they had in any way thought it through. Keith Baker has himself shown us how what the term revolution came to mean in and after 1789 was something quite different from what it had meant before.[6] And if he has also shown us that Mably at least was remarkably prescient about the way it would come about, that prophetic priest exhibited no foresight on what it would lead to in the few years afterwards.[7] I have long argued – and more recently Timothy Tackett has lent persuasive support to the idea[8] – that revolutionaries were created by the Revolution, and not the other way around. It took the Revolution itself to show how much revolution might achieve, and open people's minds to unthought-of possibilities. To say that it was only possible because it was thinkable risks the implication, so easy to accept because so many subsequent revolutions have been plotted and planned for, that those involved in the great prototype knew in advance what they wanted and how they wanted to get it.

It is true that large numbers of people had a wide range of ideas about what they did *not* want. All the work that has been done over a quarter of a century on the public sphere and what was discussed within it has emphasised how little was beyond criticism in Enlightenment France. The *cahiers* of 1789 show the huge range of dissatisfaction that existed; and all the abolitions carried out by the Constituent Assembly show how many of their habits and practices the French were glad to be rid of. Over many years studying one of those practices – venality of offices – I have been repeatedly struck by how few of venality's many old regime critics thought anything could be done to change or get rid of it. It took a revolution to bring about what had previously seemed like a utopian dream, a revolution whose scale and potentialities none of venality's critics foresaw. The same could surely be said of innumerable other institutions and habits that the French deplored in themselves. These things, happily labelled abuses by those who exultantly abolished them, were thought of as abuses even before the Revolution happened. Abolition was therefore thinkable; but the opportunity was not.

Yet, at the end of the 1780s, that opportunity happened. It happened in ways that nobody foresaw, because of contingencies that nobody could predict: the decision to intervene in America; the decision to finance that intervention without new direct taxation; the decision to present a comprehensive reform plan to an Assembly of Notables; the decision to resist their demands, etc. etc. All these, and other instances one could cite, represented choices, moments when things might have gone a different way. Accidents played their part, too: the deaths of Frederick the Great, of Vergennes, of the Dauphin; the terrible weather in 1788 and the spring of 1789. All these things, and more, combined to produce the collapse of absolute monarchy, the political old regime, in August 1788. Down with it went a whole fabric of authority and acceptance that left a sudden and enormous vacuum. Nothing could any longer be taken for granted, except that the Estates-General would meet the next year. But neither the when, the where, the how nor what would be done, were settled. The entire future was to be refashioned. It was only now that the French began to reach into their intellectual stock and confront the problems of practical change. It was only now that they began to realise that their dreams might become realities. Because it was now revealed as possible, revolution became thinkable.

But to say revolution became thinkable, even on the comprehensive scale of the French Revolution, is still not the same thing as saying that the whole of the Revolution that actually happened became thinkable. The central problems for the whole of the historiography of the Revolution, as urgent seemingly for scholars of today as they were for agonised contemporaries, are regicide and terror. (Whether they deserve that primacy is another question.) Much of the most provocative work that has appeared since the bicentenary has emphasised the inevitability of both, once the Revolution's course was set in 1789, whether we are talking about François Furet or Simon Schama on the terror, or Dale Van Kley or Lynn Hunt on regicide. Or indeed Keith Baker who assures us that in opting for a government of absolute sovereignty rather than one limited by the rights of man, the men of 1789 were '...in the long run...opting for the Terror'.[9] But let us just dwell on that long run. It was quite long: four years to regicide, five to terror, years packed with a succession of spectacular and life-transforming incidents. It was about the length of either of the two great world wars of the twentieth century, and quite as traumatic as either. Those wars had unthinkable consequences. It would have been visionary to claim in 1914 that (say) Nicholas II had opted three years in advance for the Bolshevik Revolution, or that in 1939 Hitler had opted for Stalingrad or (to go no further) that at Pearl Harbor Hirohito (or even Roosevelt) had opted for Hiroshima years down the line. A whole array of choices and chances lay in between, many of them unthinkable when those conflicts began. Why should the first four or five years of the French Revolution be any different? Those years were as full of fateful choices and accidents as the last ones of the old regime. Think of the infectious and unplanned euphoria which carried the deputies away on the night of 4 August; think of the shambles that was the flight to Varennes, a gamble that nevertheless might have succeeded if Drouet had not chanced to recognise the king; or think of the diplomatic miscalculations and misunderstandings, not to mention accidents like the death of Leopold II, which led to the outbreak of war in 1792. This is not to say that the French did not formulate their reactions to these unpredictable vicissitudes by reaching into a long-accumulated intellectual stock and (by now) revolutionary experience. As eighteenth-century people, they could only be expected to react in eighteenth-century ways – although the occasions might catalyse those ways. But their lives, like our own lives, were determined as much by chances and genuine choices as by contexts.

How could we ever have come to think otherwise? The answer goes back to the reification of the Revolution that began with that very transformation of the concept that Keith Baker has explored so carefully for us. Although revolution was now coming to be understood as something more than an eye-catching event, people continued to speak of it as if it was just that – unprecedentedly momentous perhaps, but still a single entity with a single nature or purpose – rather than the long and complex series of events and developments that it actually was. It became, as it were, a concept of special significance rather than a set of historical problems like those posed in any other period. Historians followed contemporaries in this, and it was the approach that François Furet attacked in his celebrated polemic of 1978, *Penser la Révolution française.* Yet in fact Furet himself did little other than those he was condemning, treating the Revolution (in the manner of his heroes Tocqueville and Cochin) more like a concept than a period for study. It would be absurd to deny the world-historical importance of the French Revolution. Little in history has had such far-reaching effects and ramifications. But this does not necessarily mean that we ought to study it as a unique historical phenomenon to be treated in different terms from anything else that occurred in the past. Indeed, it is precisely because it *was* so important that it needs to be looked at on cool analytical terms no different from anything else. Otherwise it becomes a largely empty pot into which we can pour almost anything we like, absolved from the professional constraints of evidence and argument.

What has always worried me about writings on the French Revolution is the proneness of its historians to determinism. Perhaps that is because I came to it as a student of the ancien régime, working on people who did not know or even guess what was about to happen to them and their world. I found the historiography of that pre-revolutionary world to be permeated by hindsight. It was a hindsight in those days, too, deeply influenced by Marxism and the categories it had imposed on our understanding of the historical processes at work. What was called revisionism was the dismantling of these teleological patterns, dispelling the shadow cast by the Revolution over its past. Revisionism, in fact, was mainly concerned with what went on before 1789 rather than after. The post-revisionism that Keith Baker and François Furet together did so much to launch in the course of the 1980s was also in its way largely about the old regime, with its concentration on the public sphere and the discourses of public life that emerged then. But it also, as Colin Lucas perceptively remarked in one of the bicentennial debates in 1989, brought the Revolution and the old regime back together again.[10] Post-revisionism was not so much concerned with explaining why the old regime disappeared, as with why the subsequent revolution took the course it did, to culminate in the shocking episodes of 1793 and 1794. It found the reasons not in the events and vicissitudes of the years between 1789 and then, but in mindsets and thought-patterns developed long before, in the public sphere since the 1750s.

In doing so, it seemed to be taking our understanding of the subject back to a certain determinism. Not, indeed, of the socio-economic sort fashionable half a century ago, but to a cultural and intellectual determinism which found explanations in logic and patterns of thought rather than in the everyday mess of human affairs, a mess we can surely recognise in our own lives, when we do not really know what is going to happen, and perhaps would be thoroughly dismayed if we did; and where we are confronted almost every day with choices great and small that are little more than gambles. This not to say that *nothing* happens that is thinkable, or that *nothing* is thinkable until it happens. Our ability to plan and conceptualise beyond our experience, to imagine the unprecedented, is one of the glories of being human. But nothing remotely like the French Revolution had ever occurred before; and while we ought certainly to study its cultural and intellectual context in order to understand it, that study is not sufficient in itself. We also need to recognise how much it owed to chance and choice; and how much of it – not all by any means, but perhaps most – only became thinkable as and when it showed itself to be possible.

CHAPTER 7

Desacralising Desacralisation

W hy was Louis XVI executed? This apparently simple question can be answered at a number of different levels. For the Convention, which almost unanimously found him guilty, he had betrayed the Nation from the beginning of the Revolution, fought against liberty, and shed the blood of his former subjects, now citizens. The indictment at his trial did not go back beyond 20 June 1789. But for the Revolution's enemies, the death of the king was the result of a much longer process. Accepting without demur the causal links claimed by the revolutionaries themselves between their programme of regeneration and the philosophy of the Enlightenment, counter-revolutionary thought blamed the latter for having planned the destruction of the monarchy throughout the eighteenth century. There had been nothing less than a philosophic plot to bring down religion and indeed the whole structure of society. Obviously monarchy could not escape the destruction. This was the argument of the most famous and certainly one of the most influential of counter-revolutionary writings, the *Mémoires pour servir à l'Histoire du Jacobinisme* (1797) of the 'mythomane jésuite'[1] Augustin de Barruel. Nothing as important as the execution of a king could have occurred without deep and prolonged preparation.

Despite the apparent common sense of this explanation, very few anti-monarchical views can be found in the thought of the Enlightenment. The supposed leaders of the philosophic plot outlined by Barruel even included a king (Frederick the Great), and Voltaire, the fawning correspondent of several monarchs and great admirer of Louis XV's final *coup de force* against his opponents in the parlements. Even Rousseau, republican dreamer though he was, did not think a republic in a land the size of France a practical possibility. Enlightenment republicanism remained theoretical, a way of reflecting on politics in general rather than a programme for anti-monarchical action. It only became a source of action during the Revolution itself, as it became increasingly clear that the king was unwilling to accept all that the National Assembly demanded of him. It was only then that the French began to draw systematically on the range of republican ideas emanating from the Enlightenment.

But if it proves scarcely possible to demonstrate that Enlightenment thought had undermined the foundations of monarchy before the Revolution, were there other trends undermining them in different ways? This has been the view, over the last few decades, of a growing number of historians, most of them not French, who represent what has been called the 'cultural turn' in historical studies. According to them, a deeper source for the fate of Louis XVI can be found in the 'desacralisation' of the monarchy under the successors of Louis XIV. As the editors of one American collection[2] have put it: 'if we can understand how the king's body became desacralized, we can understand why Louis XVI lost his head'.

The idea of a desacralised monarchy goes back to the researches of Dale Van Kley during the seventies of the last century. Having shown, in a brilliant book,[3] that the destruction of the Jesuits in France owed nothing (whatever they claimed) to the philosophers of the Enlightenment and almost everything to Jansenists in the Parlement of Paris, Van Kley argued that the 'unraveling' of the whole ancien régime could be explained by the effect of religious controversies rather than by philosophic criticism.[4] In a book on the stabbing of Louis XV by Damiens in 1757, he uncovered much popular grumbling, if not plotting, against the king's person, and attributed it to the diffuse influence of controversies surrounding the Bull *Unigenitus*. Historians must, he argued, 'hearken to the popular ground tremors first discernible beneath the refusal of sacraments controversy, which anticipate the seeming ease with which the French dispensed with their monarch in 1792'.[5] Several years later, Jeffrey Merrick devoted a whole book to the desacralisation of the French monarchy in the eighteenth century, emphasising in his turn the conflicts over *Unigenitus*, but adding hostility towards toleration for Protestants. He concluded that these 'disputes desacralized the monarchy by disrupting the conjunction of religion and politics, discrediting divine ordination, and secularizing citizenship'.[6] More recently still, Van Kley, while accepting the Protestant dimension, once more stressed the fundamental importance of 'Jansenism's long inherent tendency to desacralize everything between God and the individual conscience, divine-right monarchy not excepted.'[7]

At the same time, these perspectives have chimed in with another approach which goes back to studies carried on over more than 40 years by Robert Darnton into seditious *libelles* and clandestine literature in the later eighteenth century. 'It seems clear,' he concludes,[8] 'that the public's respect for the monarchy plummeted in the mid-eighteenth century...Much of the discontent became attached to the king's private life, which fed "public noises" at the very time when the king lost touch with the public and abandoned some of the key rituals of kingship' such as touching for scrofula, which he gave up in 1738. 'In short, by tampering with the sacred, in both royal and personal rituals, Louis XV seems to have ruptured the lines of legitimacy that bound the people to the crown.'[9] French scholars such as Arlette Farge[10] and Roger Chartier[11] subsequently reached similar conclusions.

It is an impressive list of authorities, and a powerful range of evidence and argument. And yet, anyone who studies the final years of the ancien régime might be quite surprised to hear of a king inspiring no respect or reverence in his subjects. Even at the moment of Louis XVI's execution, the crowd rushed forward to steep their handkerchiefs in his blood. Anguished disagreements also preceded the fatal vote which condemned 'Capet' to death. One might almost suggest that a truly desacralised king did not need to be executed, because without sacrality such a gesture would have no symbolic point... For Saint-Just, no king could reign innocently. Could it not be said, in contrast, that nobody wearing a crown could completely lack some form of sacrality? However that may be, a reading of the *cahiers* of 1789 and of the rhetoric of the pre-revolutionary crisis gives a very clear impression of a king still revered, loved by his subjects, accorded a majesty which was often described as sacred.[12] It appears that Louis XVI, right up to the Revolution and perhaps some way into it, was scarcely tainted by the misdeeds of his grandfather, and remained as he had been seen at the moment of his coronation in 1775, when men broke down and wept to behold him, the mystic successor of St. Louis, and accepted as such by most of his subjects.

This sacred descent was part of the official doctrine of the monarchy. But this does not necessarily mean that the ideological apparatus surrounding the monarchy was understood in all its amplitude by those who lived under its rule. Not many historians of monarchical ideologies fail to cite the words of Bossuet who under Louis XIV vaunted the semi-divine character of the king of France's authority. The interest shown by recent historians in monarchical ceremonial, whether at the coronation or when kings were buried,[13] has emphasised the complexity of the ideologies of the monarchical state, and the depth of symbolism underpinning every gesture at these moments when divine right was transmitted. There was no shortage of ideologues at the time to analyse the significance of these public dramas; not to mention modern cultural exegetes. It might even be suggested that the full and complex ideology of divine right absolute monarchy, as it was elaborated at the end of the sixteenth and throughout the seventeenth century, was an attempt to *re*sacralise the monarchy after the shocks of the Wars of Religion, not to mention two regicides. But at the same time we should ask how much of it the king's ordinary subjects understood. Desacralisation presupposes a prior sacralisation, and subsequent loss of beliefs formerly accepted. Yet nothing leads us to believe that the great majority of the subjects of Louis XV or the young Louis XVI had a deep or even superficial knowledge of the doctrinal elements of the king's 'sacral' authority, only to reject them with a sort of disgust as the eighteenth century progressed. The reverence of most subjects was far simpler and more instinctive – yet at the same time more flexible.

It often seems to me, from the perspective of a country where monarchy still exists, that citizens of republican cultures tend to overestimate the awe and understanding of monarchical symbolism that subjects of monarchies possess. A well-established monarchy such as that of old regime France, where there is no serious alternative, can tolerate a level of indifference, not to say ignorance, about the established norms of political obligation which would seem very troubling in a republic. Nor should we overestimate the importance of the disloyal talk of which the desacralising thesis makes so much. The authorities disapproved, of course: that was why anything that came to the ears of the police was followed up. But instances only cropped up by chance, except in the wake of serious incidents such as the Damiens episode, when more systematic enquiries seemed to be required. And significantly enough, subversive talk (*mauvais discours*) and vague threats against the king's life could be found long before the reign of Louis XV. Arlette Farge discovered them even in the reign of Louis XIV himself.[14] Nor did she see anything in them that was truly threatening, for the institution of monarchy at least. Subjects who denounced the king, casually called him a bugger, or even talked of killing him, were not necessarily against monarchy as such: what they were against was a particular king who they thought had betrayed the obligations of his office. Even more so in the case of actual regicides. Whether it was Clément in 1589, Ravaillac in 1610 or Damiens in 1757, the assassin was stabbing a man whom he thought unworthy of the crown. In other words the king had failed in his most sacred duty, and as it were desacralised himself. He was attacked to *restore* the sacred character of the throne and in no way out of a loss of respect for the institution of monarchy.

Even the personal desacralisation of Louis XV took quite a time. It is often dated from his refusal in 1738 to go to confession, and therefore to touch for scrofula, not being in a state of grace. And yet Louis XIV had never felt prevented from performing this miracle despite awareness of his numerous sins. Perhaps Louis XV was *more* scrupulous than his predecessor with respect to this most sacred of his attributes? He abstained from the sacraments because of his sinful and debauched way of life; but a debauched lifestyle had done nothing to damage the reputation of Henry IV among his subjects, nor indeed that of the young Louis XIV. The latter's reputation suffered far more when in later life he became the faithful husband of Mme de Maintenon, who was devout but seen as too ambitious.[15] Even the early mistresses of Louis XV seem not to have damaged him; otherwise would there have been such an outburst of joy at the Well-Beloved's recovery of health after his famous illness at Metz in 1744? It was only with the arrival of Mme de Pompadour that his private life began to arouse scandal, and to give rise to improbable rumours like that of 1750, suggesting children being kidnapped so that the king could cure his illnesses by bathing in their blood.[16] After that, too, there was a long series of disasters: the quarrel over the refusal of sacraments, the diplomatic revolution and its calamitous consequences in the Seven Years' War, endless further debauchery, ever more sordid, culminating in the rise of a recognised woman of the streets, Mme Dubarry, more or less coinciding with Chancellor Maupeou's attack on the sovereign courts and the fiscal extortions of the Abbé Terray. It was no surprise that such a discredited king should die unlamented; but the general enthusiasm which greeted his young successor showed that the institution of monarchy had scarcely been tarnished by the unworthy behaviour of one particular monarch. There was a renewal of hope, to which Louis XVI willingly responded, whether by removing the tyrannical 'triumvirate' of ministers who had led the old monarch astray, or by restoring the ceremony of touching for scrofula (with more than 2,400 sufferers turning up) following the coronation.

It is true that the reign of Louis XVI proved unlucky. Although France revenged herself on the British by helping their American colonies to achieve their independence, the cost of this conflict brought about the collapse of the ancien régime. And although the personal life of the king remained pure and unblemished, the absence of children before 1778, and no dauphin before 1781, left him open to some ridicule. But it was easier to fix the blame for this on the Austrian queen, brought to France to cement a reversal of alliances which the Seven Years' War had proved to be disastrous. The natural frivolity of Marie-Antoinette and the extravagance of her favourite friends and courtiers made her the same sort of target as mistresses had been under previous kings, even if she also served as a sort of lightning conductor shielding her husband from more direct criticism. It was only after 1785, quite late therefore, that the queen's influence began to be perceived as pernicious, following the mismanaged affair of the diamond necklace and the purchase for her of the palace of Saint-Cloud. It used to be argued that a stream of hostile *libelles* against her and the king's younger brothers served during all this time to undermine royal prestige; but the recent researches of Simon Burrows have shown that most of the broadsides so often invoked were not published until after the Revolution was under way.[17] It was mainly about the already notorious debauchery of Louis XV, now safely dead, that the French public continued to be titillated under his successor. And during the pre-revolutionary crisis of 1787–88, it was 'ministerial despotism', seen as misleading a benevolent king, which incensed most pamphleteers. As noted earlier, the *cahiers* of 1789 were full of professions of faith in the king's good intentions. Even after all his suspicious hesitations and u-turns of May, June and July 1789, at the end of the euphoric night of 4 August, to cries of *Vive le Roi!,* the deputies of the National Assembly proclaimed Louis XVI 'Restorer of French Liberties' and ordered a medal struck with that legend.

In the light of all these doubts, the idea of a desacralised monarchy looks poorly framed, and underpinned by questionable presuppositions. At a general level it assumes that any important historical event needs long preparation to become possible – a fundamental but profoundly debateable tenet of the cultural turn in present-day historical studies.[18] Secondly it presupposes a fairly uniform level of reception for monarchical ideology, as if every subject of the Sun King, literate or not, knew and accepted the doctrines of Bodin or Bossuet, on which their children or grandchildren subsequently turned their backs. Finally it implies, perhaps rather unreflectively, that the goal of the Revolution from the very beginning was to destroy monarchy, and that it should be regarded, to adapt the famous formula of Georges Clemenceau, as a republican block. This viewpoint enjoyed the prestigious endorsement of François Furet,[19] at least later in his career: but to accept it risks neglecting the unforeseeable in revolutionary events.

Nobody in 1789, not even the most disenchanted of subjects, dreamed of bringing down the monarchy. The original political project of the Revolution was to turn an absolute monarchy into a constitutional one. Even under a regime where legitimate political authority would emanate from the will of the Nation rather than the grace of God, the constituents never envisaged being able to replace at will a king genetically designated by divine providence. It was the increasingly evident reluctance of Louis XVI to accept the reforms of the Constituent Assembly which made his fellow citizens begin to doubt whether this monarch, formerly absolute, could ever be the sincere head of a state governed through representative institutions. And it was the king's attempt to escape, in the flight to Varennes on 21 June 1791, which unleashed a republican movement culminating on 10 August 1792, and which opened the way to his trial and execution. In other words, it was the dynamic of events, and not some prior desacralisation of monarchy, which led Louis XVI to the scaffold on 21 January 1793.

This is not to imply that no sort of desacralisation had occurred over the eighteenth century. Whether it is called that, or secularisation, or (unsatisfactory though the term is[20]) dechristianisation, it is widely agreed that over that time profound changes took place in religious practice and the attitudes of the faithful. This was the background to revolutionary attempts to refound the organisation of the church through the Civil Constitution of the Clergy. Although planned as *aggiornamento* rather than an attack on religion, the attempt to impose the Civil Constitution was nevertheless the fundamental rupture of the Revolution which lent focus to all the discontents aroused since 1789, including those of the king. Even though he gave his assent to the Civil Constitution, and even to the oath demanded of the clergy to demonstrate acceptance of the new order, Louis XVI rejected both *in petto*. He spent the spring of 1791 avoiding confession or attendance at Mass conducted by a priest who had sworn the oath, well aware at the same time of the pope's hostility to the new religious order. In other words, it was a religious dilemma that made the king decide to attempt escape.[21] In this sense, the fall of the monarchy might yet be seen as the result of a certain sort of desacralisation – but not one traceable long beforehand. Rather it derived from a Revolution whose origins lay elsewhere, and whose dynamic came mostly from its own day to day evolution.

Callet's ceremonial portrait of Louis XVI, an engraving kept by George Washington at Mount Vernon (See p. 132)

CHAPTER 8

The French Revolution and Monarchy

The French Revolution is one of that handful of historical events that everybody knows, or thinks they know,
something about, even if what they know is culled largely
from *A Tale of Two Cities* or *The Scarlet Pimpernel*; and these days,
not the books either, but rather the films of the books. One image
dominates these snapshot perceptions: the guillotine, that uniquely
gory, inhuman, mechanical decapitator, the chosen instrument of
social resentment and class terror, surrounded by the screaming
mob, and grim and vengeful lower-class harridans, knitting, and
ticking off the aristocratic heads as they rolled into the basket.
Everybody knows this. Everybody has seen a version, or several versions, of this lurid scene, and has never forgotten it, and recognises
it instantly when it recurs. It *is* the French Revolution. They also
know, though perhaps rather more vaguely, that the most illustrious of the aristocratic victims of terror were a king and queen.
They know it was a Louis, though probably not which one – there
were so many. They probably do know that his queen was called
Marie-Antoinette, much more of a one-off name to remember. If
they know that, they probably also know (though quite errone-
ously) that she made one very silly remark: *let them eat cake*. Silly
it undoubtedly was, but surely (so the thinking proceeds) not hei-
nous enough to cost her her head. Such a terrible penalty for such

an innocent quip. And so the word slips out: *innocence*. It is the catalyst that makes the drama of the guillotine work. Whatever its victims had done, they did not deserve *this*. What they did deserve never then enters into it.

A further mental leap follows: if the French Revolution killed the king and his consort, then the Revolution must have been in essence anti-monarchical. This was certainly the reflex of the Duke of Edinburgh who, explaining Queen Elizabeth II's refusal to attend the celebrations to mark the 200th anniversary of the fall of the Bastille in 1989, declared that a movement which murdered monarchs was not something to celebrate. President François Mitterrand knew as well as anybody what dangerous associations the memory of the Revolution had: that was why he emphasised that the Bicentenary was celebrating 200 years of the Rights of Man, something that could be completely separated from the guillotine, and terror, and regicide. But it was no good. People refused to take the Revolution apart in their minds; and the most successful historians of the bicentenary year were those who most clearly proclaimed that the Revolution was all of a bloodthirsty piece, and could not be meaningfully disaggregated – François Furet in French, Simon Schama in English.[1]

But was the French Revolution anti-monarchical from the start? Only, it seems to me, in a very restricted sense, and one that constituted no necessary threat to the persons of Louis XVI and his queen. What the French unquestionably were against in 1789 was *absolute* monarchy. They wanted representative government. They believed that they were overtaxed, over governed and misgoverned too. The crisis out of which the Revolution emerged, after all, arose because the state's finances were out of control, and ministers admitted as much. Now, in objective terms, much of this was Louis XVI's fault. As an absolute monarch, he took all the financial decisions on every great matter of state. He was, therefore, directly responsible for France's fateful involvement in the American War of Independence; and for the overspending that followed. Louis XVI's insistence that he understood finance (so clearly brought out in John Hardman's recent biography[2]) and his consequent refusal to surrender financial oversight to anyone else, was surely one of the more important precipitants of the old regime's final crisis. Yet his subjects do not appear to have blamed him for any of this. Hardly a note of criticism against the king personally is heard before July 1789. There was much joking and lampooning, of course, about his sexual incompetence; and historians recently have made a good deal of this, arguing for a decline in respect for the monarchy, if not a positive desacralisation.[3] But the sexual habits and personal inadequacies of French monarchs had been a subject for lampoons and popular jokes since at least the time of Henry III, back in the sixteenth century. Interestingly, it is historians born and brought up in republics who have made the most of the desacralisation idea: those born subjects of a monarch know that sovereigns can take a huge amount of criticism and ridicule without monarchy itself coming remotely under threat. What is most striking about the atmosphere in France in the late 1780s is the almost touching faith that most of Louis XVI's subjects retained in their king's benevolence and good intentions. In a totally traditional way, they blamed ministers and courtiers for everything that had gone wrong, for misleading the king and abusing his credulity. If the king knew the facts, the message comes through again and again, he would not allow these things to happen; he would ensure that justice was done, he would protect his people. The appeal of representative government was that it would give him this true information. The purpose of representation was to control ministers, not the king; to outflank their control of access to the sovereign by putting him into direct touch with the concerns of his subjects. That was, after all, the historical role of the assembly which all opponents of the government were calling for from 1787 to 1789, the Estates-General. Elections to these bodies had traditionally been accompanied, as this one was, by the drawing-up of *cahiers*, grievances lists precisely intended to bring the complaints of his subjects directly to the King's ears. It is largely on the basis of these *cahiers* that these claims can be made about what the French thought of their monarch in 1789.

The original aim of the French Revolution, therefore, was not to destroy monarchy, but to change an absolute monarchy into a constitutional one. Popular antagonism throughout the struggles of 1788 and the first half of 1789 was directed against the nobility and clergy, the so-called 'privileged orders', rather than against the king. Although Louis XVI was dismally ineffective in holding the ring in these conflicts, it was largely perceived that he *was* holding the ring rather than taking sides with the privileged. If the first suspicion about his conduct arose over the troop movements revoked after the defiance of Paris on 14 July, goodwill towards the king survived the crisis. Only three weeks later, the destruction of the old social order on the night of 4 August concluded to cries of *Vive le Roi!* and the order that a commemorative medal be struck, proclaiming Louis XVI 'Restorer of French Liberties'.

It was only when the National Assembly turned, in the following weeks, to drafting the rules for a constitutional monarchy, that the problems began. Almost the first question they confronted was that of whether the king should have a veto on legislation, and if so, whether it should be permanent or merely delaying. When the king appeared hesitant to accept the ultimate decision in favour of delaying power only, the result was the march of the Parisian women to Versailles in the first days of October. Scenes of riot in the palace were followed by the famous procession back to Paris, which, in terms of the impact of the French Revolution on monarchy in general, was one of its most decisive occurrences. For, whether they applauded the event or deplored it, all onlookers could agree with Richard Price's famous description of the procession back to Paris as subjects leading their king in triumph. The king had been taken prisoner in his own palace, and humiliated. He was no longer a free agent. He had not even, like Charles I, been defeated in battle. He had simply surrendered himself, and his power, to a mob.

These events broke the mystique of monarchy far more decisively than Louis' execution 39 months later. After all, French kings had been killed before: there was Henry III and Henry IV, and as recently as 1757 a would-be assassin had stabbed Louis XV. Like mocking and lampooning the monarch, regicide was nothing new in French history. Louis XVI was not the first king to be put on trial either, of course. That dubious distinction belonged to Charles I of England – by whom Louis XVI was fascinated long before it was conceivable that he might one day share the same fate.[4] Nor was Louis XVI the first monarch to be killed by his subjects even in the eighteenth century. Many suspected that that was what had happened to Charles XII of Sweden, although the issue remains open to this day.[5] Most people thought Catherine the Great had murdered her husband, Peter III; and in the spring of 1792, at a masked ball in Stockholm, Gustav III was assassinated by dissident noblemen. Interestingly, however, with his dying words Gustav placed the blame not on the aristocrats with whom he had been in conflict for a number of years, but on *Jacobins* – friends, or agents of the French Revolution. At this moment, Louis XVI was still on the throne of France, but here was a dying king stating the conviction that revolutionary France was the natural enemy of all monarchs.

That conviction surely went back to Louis XVI's captivity in Paris which began on 6 October 1789. It showed how vulnerable kingly power could be, and that there was no necessity for ordinary people to be cowed by it. It made people think about the nature of monarchical authority, how it was best maintained, and how it might be lost; it made them think about what it was for, whether it was necessary, and if so, why. All these were questions scarcely addressed in the eighteenth century until then. Of course, there had been plenty of discussion about the nature of monarchical authority, and its legitimate limits, but nobody seriously thought of turning any monarchy into a republic. Republics, the orthodoxy was, could only work in small states, like the Greek cities of classical antiquity. Most contemporary republics were certainly of that sort. Even the biggest, the Dutch Republic, was in reality a loose federation of smaller units. So ingrained was this sense that large countries could not work as republics, that it took the intervention of an iconoclastic outsider, Tom Paine, to convince even the American rebels against George III, in his pamphlet *Common Sense*, that they could do without a king. Even then the experience of the Articles of Confederation convinced many Americans of the need for some sort of monarch – which in some senses the American president is during his term of office. Although the American republic worked well enough to secure its independence, as with so much about eighteenth-century America, Europeans simply said *it couldn't happen here*, and ignored the example, however interesting they found it.

It was, therefore, the captivity of Louis XVI in Paris, and the way the National Assembly recast the nation's institutions without reference to him, which convinced people that republicanism was a viable proposition for an important European state. Whether onlookers welcomed or deplored the prospect depended on how they viewed the circumstances which had brought about the captivity. Edmund Burke, launching a belated debate on the Revolution with his *Reflections* of 1790, clearly abominated the idea. He was first stung into writing precisely by Price's celebrations of the October Days, which Burke saw as the work of the swinish multitude. For Burke, the French monarchy was a natural growth, something to be improved, but treasured, rather than abandoned at the behest of a mob. He was outraged at the insult offered to a queen whose youthful charm had captured his imagination on a visit to Paris years before. Naturally, monarchs, with the possible exception of Emperor Leopold II, were horrified by the prospect of Louis XVI marooned in what seemed a hostile capital, unable to influence in any way the fate of his country – or so at least they presumed, since after the October Days he never raised the slightest demur at any piece of legislation put to him for sanction by the National Assembly. What Louis XVI himself thought also had to be presumed, since he said very little to anyone, as had always been his way. Most of the evidence we have for what he thought comes from Marie-Antoinette, who had her own agenda, not necessarily the same as his. What finally dispelled the last doubts was his attempt to escape from his metropolitan captivity in the Flight to Varennes in June 1791. None could doubt, after that, that this king was unreconciled to what had happened to him and his power since 1789; and whereas what he really intended by the flight remains a matter for scholarly disagreement,[6] everybody at the time, on all sides, thought his intention was to escape the country entirely, and only return accompanied by the armed cohorts of foreign monarchs. The capture, and the return of the fugitives to Paris, was the October Days all over again, but (as it were) in technicolour. Popular republicanism in France now came out into the open, while rulers abroad began to talk about military intervention to restore the king of France to his rightful position and prerogatives.

From then on, the French monarchy was doomed. True, the fiction was elaborated that the royal family had been kidnapped, the king was reinstated, and accepted the new constitution. He remained on the throne until 10 August 1792. But hardly anyone by now believed that a constitutional monarchy with him at the head of it could work, or was even worth making work. He himself continued to dream, if no longer of escape, at least of rescue. He welcomed war in the spring of 1792 as the opportunity to bring that moment closer, even though he knew that his opponents only wanted it in order to bring him down. As a result, further humiliations were in store, even before the monarchy was overthrown. On 20 June, for instance, after he had refused to rescind vetoes on legislation against presumed traitors, a mob penned him in a corner at the palace, and amid much jeering and coarse insults, forced him to wear the red cap of liberty and to drink the Nation's health. With dignity and resignation, he did so: but refused to yield on the veto. At a late stage, he was beginning to acquire some stature in adversity, assets he would build on further at his trial. On that occasion, again with calm and dignity, he claimed either innocence or ignorance as each charge was read to him. These displays of stoicism in the face of mortal danger, carried through to his behaviour on the scaffold itself, did more for his reputation, and that of monarchy itself, than all the stumbles and fumbles, the gaucheries and the stupidities, that marked his public behaviour over much of his reign. As a reigning monarch, Louis XVI had always lacked the desirable presence and dignity. Faced with martyrdom for monarchy, he suddenly acquired it. Perhaps he had learned something from all that reading about Charles I.

By the time the execution happened, nobody outside France was surprised. It was all that could be expected from a movement that had consistently humiliated the king ever since October 1789. Once the monarchy had been overthrown, amid considerable bloodshed as the Swiss Guards attempted to defend the Tuileries Palace against the forces of the Paris Commune, the fate of the former king seemed a foregone conclusion. They would execute him. Nothing else seemed safe for the new republic. The people of Paris certainly thought that, as did large numbers of the

Convention now ruling France. Yet close inspection reveals that a large number of people were not in favour of executing him. While the Convention agreed at his trial almost unanimously that he was guilty of the charges brought against him, the decision to execute him passed, famously, by a single vote; and almost half the Convention subsequently voted for a reprieve.[7] Here were deputies who thought it would do no good to execute an adversary already defeated; that it would be needlessly provocative; that it would make the National Convention seem the tool of the bloodthirsty populace of Paris, which only three weeks after the fall of the monarchy had massacred hundreds of inmates of the capital's prisons; and that it would make it infinitely more difficult to restore a monarchy later. Nobody made this last point in their speeches on the question. In the atmosphere of late 1792, it would have been suicidal. But we can be certain that it was uppermost in the minds of many. This is the great paradox of the French Revolution's impact on monarchy. For every person whom it convinced that kingship could, and should, be dispensed with, there were many more (even if they were not in a majority in the Convention) who found that the whole experience demonstrated the *necessity* of monarchy.

Nobody at all had doubted it at the start. One wonders whether, if the king had been somebody other than the wooden and unimaginative Louis XVI, married to a lethally silly woman, it would ever have been called into doubt at all. The fatal problem was that a reluctant king, or more often, a king presumed to be reluctant, could only be made compliant by unleashing the Parisian populace against him; and that made mob rule seem the only possible alternative to monarchy. Once he had been brought to Paris, it was assumed that this ploy would not be needed again; and the National Assembly blithely continued drafting its constitution, assuming that Louis had learned his lesson and would not drag his feet again. It took him for granted, and only learned its mistake when he tried to escape. In the aftermath of Varennes, overt republicanism surfaced; and the mask it wore was that of the Parisian people, whom the constitution makers had planned to exclude from all say under their constitutional monarchy. Now they realised how right they had been: a king was the surest ally of men of property against the destructive envy of those who had nothing. He symbolised authority and hierarchy as nothing else could.

So the months after the *débacle* of Varennes had seen the first serious attempts to conciliate and win over Louis XVI to the virtues of the constitution, by men who saw that France could not do without a king. With the king they had, unfortunately, it was too late. He was beyond winning over, embittered by all that they had allowed to happen to him – thereby confirming all the worst suspicions that republicans had of him. So the country polarised into those who felt that the Revolution could never be safe so long as this king sat on the French throne, and those who believed that the gains of the Revolution would never be stably established without a monarchy to endow them with some permanence and continuity. If the execution of the monarch whom his enemies loved to call Louis the Last was intended to settle this conflict, it signally failed to do so. Within two months of the execution, a royalist rebellion had broken out in the Vendée that would rumble on for a decade. If all that the persistence of royalism, and the support given to it by an ever-widening circle of foreign enemies, including the British, did in the short run was to provoke further gratuitous anti-monarchical gestures, like the execution of Marie-Antoinette (after a ludicrous trial and a range of farcical charges that nobody except Lynn Hunt could take seriously[8]), none of this lent any real strength to French republicanism. The first two years of the French republic, after all, were marked by the horrific episode with whose imagery this essay began: the Terror. Systematic massacre was scarcely an alluring advertisement for politics without a king. The moment the Terror was over, accordingly, men began to think of a restoration. It seems clear that among men of property at least, there was a heavy majority in favour of a monarchy from this time right down to Napoleon's seizure of power in 1799. The results of successive elections, and the measures taken by the Directory to annul them, show that plainly enough. Their only problem was their candidate. Louis XVII, Louis XVI's last remaining son, looked ideal. Still a child, and in captivity, he could be brought up as a copy-book constitutional monarch through a carefully controlled education. But he died in 1795. That left Louis XVI's brothers, and within weeks the elder, in proclaiming himself Louis XVIII, had thrown his chance away with the Declaration of Verona, in which he pledged, if restored, to dismantle the entire work of the Revolution since 1789. Once again, the proverbial stupidity of the Bourbons had snatched defeat from the jaws of victory. In the face of Louis XVIII's intransigence, France's weary constitution-makers had no alternative but to go ahead with a republican form of government, whatever its unfortunate and bloodthirsty associations.

It never worked; but despite that Louis XVIII had to wait another 20 years before he sat securely on the throne of France. The reason was, of course, that Napoleon had captured that lost monarchist constituency which the pretender had turned his back on at Verona. After four years in which a revamped republic, while avoiding further terror, signally failed to deliver the stability which royalists believed only a monarch could provide, the French propertied classes handed themselves over to a successful general who promised to impose order and respect the Revolution's gains, even if he offered no guarantees for representative government. Napoleon did all that a king was expected to do, leaving the only arguments of those who still preferred a Bourbon to him, as mere arguments of sentiment. When Louis XVIII was eventually restored, at the hands of foreign victors, only a handful of Frenchmen saw this primarily as a victory of some mystic legitimacy. It was simply that there was nobody else.

The French Revolution, therefore, though it showed for the first time that a republic in a large European state was a practical possibility rather than a classical dream, failed to offer the prospect of such a republic working, except by Terror or (as between 1795 and 1799) repeated *coups d'état*. It was scarcely an encouraging prospect. So the Revolution, though it consistently humiliated and then destroyed a king, did not destroy the appeal of monarchy. On the contrary, it reinforced that appeal with a terrifying spectacle of what life without one could be like. It was a lesson that the nineteenth century was to learn thoroughly. Many new states were established during the century after 1789, but hardly any were established as republics. It had become more axiomatic than ever that a viable state needed a monarch – even one, like Belgium or Italy, created with the help of insurrection. Republics in nineteenth-century Europe were fleeting and tumultuous, and therefore tended to underline the lessons of the 1790s. Only in France did a durable republic eventually establish itself, almost a hundred years after the Revolution; and only then because another Bourbon, missing his chance according to an unerring family tradition, refused once again to compromise with the Revolution's legacy even though a gesture would have given him the throne.

So in the end, the French monarchy at least was destroyed by the Revolution; even if, as anyone who looks at the constitution of the Fifth Republic can see, the monarchical reflex in French political life remains powerful. Although it reinforced the case for monarchy as a general principle in Europe, the Revolution changed the sources of its strength. Monarchy now appealed not because it had always been there, and not because it was ordained by God, but because it was a symbol and guarantee of the social order. The French Revolution, and the fate of Louis XVI, largely destroyed its mystical appeal. Nineteenth-century monarchies flourished because they worked, not because they were right. Monarchy now had to work to earn the respect it received. It could no longer expect it as its due. Burke saw that as early as 1790 'never, never more, shall we behold that generous loyalty to rank... that proud submission, that dignified obedience, that subordination of the heart, which kept alive, even in servitude itself, the spirit of an exalted freedom'. In the post-revolutionary age, one monarch could always be replaced by another. Who needed a Louis so long as there was a Napoleon? Of course, new-age monarchs tried to decorate themselves with traditional trappings. Napoleon gave himself a lavish coronation, and eventually, like Louis XIV and Louis XVI before him, married a Habsburg. He set up a court, created a form of nobility to people it. That was what people expected kings to do. The one thing they no longer expected them to do was take it all seriously enough to think that they ruled by divine right. When Charles X, who began his reign with a lavish traditional coronation at Reims, looked like trying to revive the monarchy of the ancien régime, he did not last six years. The Revolution of 1830 summarily bundled him out and installed another, less tradition-bound ruler in his place, Louis-Philippe, the umbrella-king: a new ruler for a new age.

But it was not simply mystical posturings that ruined Charles X. They were all of a piece with more profound misjudgements. His dream was not simply to restore the mystique of his murdered brother's monarchy, but also much of his power. What really triggered the Revolution of 1830 was the fear that the king and his friends wanted to take France back beyond the Revolution to the absolute monarchy of the ancien régime. For the Revolution had destroyed that, too. Its original aim had been to substitute a constitutional monarchy for an absolute one. In the short term it failed: in the longer term, however, it made constitutional monarchy the only acceptable sort: that is, a monarchy that reigned in open, and, to one degree or another, institutional co-operation with its subjects. Napoleon, the first monarch to rule France after the death of Louis XVI, could afford to ignore this lesson, ruling as he did on the capital of having restored stability, and of military success – although even he had some cardboard representative institutions. But in all sorts of ways, he was exceptional. After 1789, other monarchs had to learn that they needed social allies, that the forces of order had to be conciliated with some say in how things were run. The age of absolutism was over. Kings who tried to perpetuate it did so at their peril.

It was not simply the example of what happened to Louis XVI, however, that taught these lessons. It was also the fact that every monarch in Europe saw his territory invaded, plundered, carved up, and often redistributed by the French, and sometimes several times over, between 1792 and 1814. Crushing military defeat, deposition or expulsion from territories often ruled for generations, could scarcely fail to dent the prestige and authority of the rulers undergoing such traumas. Eighteenth-century warfare had been about bargaining and balancing off the recognised rights of adversaries. Revolutionary and Napoleonic conflict was about winner taking all. Some monarchies did not survive this more brutal atmosphere. The most hoary and illustrious victim was the Holy Roman Empire itself, along with many a smaller German principality. But those that did resurface were often barely recognisable, and as a result their rulers had to rebuild their shattered authority on new, more utilitarian foundations. Napoleon, as heir to the Revolution, forced all rulers with whom he came into conflict to do things his way, and create their own authority anew. Like him, they did it not by appealing to their prescriptive rights and ancient, God-given authority, but to the material interests of their subjects. They now needed to win support, to earn it, rather than assume it.

Only one monarchy survived these upsets unscathed, and that was of course the Crown of Great Britain. There were, certainly, republican stirrings after Paine's *Rights of Man* was published, and in Ireland in 1798 there was a full-scale rebellion in favour of republican independence. Once war with the ancestral enemy broke out, however, the British rallied to their monarchy and lent fraternity and assistance to the French pretender. But George III and his ancestors had ruled, ever since 1688, with the co-operation and consent of their greater subjects; and for at least a century there had been no absolute, divine-right monarchy to challenge in the island state. And that was largely because the islanders had chopped off their own king's head a century and a half earlier.

Lafayette by Jean-Antoine Houdon,
courtesy of the Virginia General Assembly

CHAPTER 9

The American Revolution and the European Nobility

There are many ways of defining the American Revolution, as there are of defining the French one, or any other.
Gallons of ink have been spilled in elaborating such
definitions, and in arguing about them. But, unlike the French
Revolution and many another, there is at least no disagreement
about what the American Revolution was at the outset. It was the
renunciation of a king. Nothing so clear-cut marks the beginning
of the French Revolution; and the nearest equivalent, the seizure of
national sovereignty by a self-styled National Assembly on 17 June
1789, is often drowned in the narrative of so many other momentous events. The 14th July is the date commemorated today, even
though the importance of what happened on that day is more
symbolic than substantial. But with 4 July 1776 there can be no
ambiguity. Renouncing allegiance to George III was an unequivocal act. Congress was declaring a republic.

That was a revolution in itself. The only remotely comparable
precedent in European consciousness was the Dutch Republic's
renunciation of Philip II of Spain in the sixteenth century. But of
course this revolutionary act was only a beginning. What did not
having a king imply? It took half a generation for the Americans to
work out the basic implications, and this process (most historians
would agree) constitutes the true American Revolution, which

certainly did not end when George III accepted their claim to independence in 1783. Few aspects of political, social, spiritual, or economic organisation went undebated during the first quarter century of the American Republic; and what emerged as consensual about republican life was often the result of bitterly contested choices.[1] One thing, however, seems to have been consensual throughout, a principle of republican life which nobody ever tried, or at least explicitly dared, to contest: the republic would have no nobility.

It was implicit in the Declaration of Independence itself, with its assertion of the self-evident truth that 'all men are created equal'. A year later, in their first attempt at a federal constitution, the Articles of Confederation, the states agreed, seemingly without debate, in Article VI that 'the United States in Congress assembled, nor any one of them' should 'not grant any title of nobility'.[2] Ten years after that, the same provision passed undiscussed into the Federal Constitution, under Section IX, which stated: 'No title of nobility shall be granted by the United States; and no person holding any office of profit or trust under them shall, without the consent of the Congress, accept of any present, emolument, office or title, of any kind whatever, from any king, prince, or foreign State.' Section X went on to forbid any of the individual states from granting any title of nobility either. This provision, said James Madison in that great defence of the new constitution *The Federalist* (No 44), needed no comment. And 'Nothing' wrote Alexander Hamilton in No 88, 'need be said to illustrate the importance of the prohibition of titles of nobility. This may truly be denominated the corner stone of republican government.'

The American revolutionaries derived this conviction from a wide range of sources. One of the incentives of many of their ancestors in crossing the Atlantic had been to escape the social hierarchies of old Europe. They had no desire to re-create them. And one of the first things any European visitor to America noticed was its egalitarian culture – although this was stronger in northern states than in parts of the south. Confronted with the problem of establishing a viable republic, the well-educated Founding Fathers knew that nobles and republics were natural enemies. From Machiavelli they had learned that nobilities were selfish vermin, with no public spirit.[3] From Montesquieu, a more recent analyst whom they revered unequivocally, they accepted that nobilities were inseparable from monarchy, and even under monarchs worked primarily in their own interests, pursuing honour rather than the virtue which was the spirit of true republics.[4] 'Aristocracy', it was widely agreed, was one of the greatest dangers that the United States was likely to confront as it developed. By aristocracy, it is true, they did not mean exactly the same thing as nobility, although nobility was (as it were) a strong form of it. Nor did they tend to accept the classic, Aristotelian meaning of Aristocracy as government by the best people. They meant something closer to oligarchy – the accumulation of great wealth and property in a few hands, its transfer by heredity down the generations, and the use of these resources to capture and control political power. They sought to prevent this happening by the prohibition of primogeniture and entails, a movement that swept all the states where they had previously been permitted over the 15 years after 1776.[5] Some, like John Adams, thought additionally that balanced constitutions would contain and prevent an otherwise inevitable drift towards aristocratic power.[6] But, whatever their apprehensions about how their society might later develop, the fact remains that the Founding Fathers of the American Republic had created, for the first time since antiquity, a polity in which nobles by definition had no role to play; and where, in fact, they were regarded as a fatally dangerous alien species.

Yet the process of achieving American independence was full of paradoxes. One was that independence from the rule of George III could not have been achieved, or at least not as quickly and decisively, without the help of another king, Louis XVI of France.

In recognition of this, George Washington, soon to be the first president of the new republic, placed a printed portrait of the French king in a room in his house at Mount Vernon, where it can still be seen. No less striking was the fact that this republic was helped into being by the efforts of a very wide range of European noblemen. Whether at the highest level as the advisors of kings – men like the Count de Vergennes, the French foreign secretary, or the Count de Floridablanca, his Spanish counterpart; or as ambassadors, or generals, admirals, and the officers who served under them, above all in the French army and navy; or as volunteers in the American service; in all these roles members of the European nobility played a crucial part in the Americans' struggle to establish the independence of their republic. Others cheered them on from the safe sidelines of Europe. What can they have been thinking of?

They were certainly not thinking about any implicit threat to themselves or the social order to which they belonged. They appear not to have realised, unless and until they got there, that people like themselves enjoyed no standing in America. The ministers who involved their royal masters in the American struggle were not interested in the internal structure of American society, or its values. They did worry that in helping republicans to shake off their allegiance to their legitimate monarch they were setting a bad example to subjects everywhere. No contemporary monarch is on record as positively approving the defiance of the Americans, and several were vocal in their condemnation of the rebellion. But the concern of the noble ministers who lent their masters' support to these rebels was entirely a matter of power politics. They wanted to wreck the British Empire, revenge themselves for the humiliations of the Seven Years' War, and hopefully capture the trade of the new republic for themselves. They showed no interest in the principles for which the 13 colonies rebelled, and only agreed to recognise their independence after the rebels had shown, at Saratoga, that they were capable of defeating a professional British army on their own. European statesmen calculated that the new republic would be distant and weak, but that its loss to Great Britain would destroy the ambition of the 'Modern Carthage' to control Europe's links with the rest of the world.

Revenge on the British was also a powerful sentiment suffusing the French armed forces, who still tended to regard the islanders as military upstarts who had failed to recognise the 'natural' hegemony to which French arms were entitled. A great deal of recent scholarship has emphasised the outburst of affronted patriotism in France following the conclusion of peace in 1763.[7] French naval officers burned to use the fleet rebuilt by Choiseul to avenge the defeats of Lagos and Quiberon; not to mention reversing its relative neglect since Choiseul's downfall in 1770. Their military counterparts, thoroughly shaken up and reorganised, ever more radically, down to the ministry of the Count de Saint-Germain at the very moment when the Americans were declaring independence, longed for the opportunity to see whether all this upheaval had been worthwhile for restoring the honour of French arms.

Besides, it would give them something glorious and exciting to do. These officers saw themselves as made to fight, not to rot away in provincial garrison towns. War was their vocation; and we should never underestimate the steady, relentless pressure they exerted on all governments to give them the chance to do what they thought they were best at. And this was not simply the officers in service. War meant an expansion of the forces, more jobs and commands for everybody with military credentials and ambitions. Even before the French, the Spaniards, and eventually the Dutch, began to expand their official forces and to take their fleets out of mothballs, noblemen all over Europe were seeing the American rebellion as a personal opportunity of the sort not currently available in the old continent. On the assumption that the commercial, unmilitary colonists had no experience of fighting or military organisations, they flocked across the Atlantic to offer their services – in effect as mercenaries. The most famous and iconic of these figures is of course Lafayette, who flouted direct royal orders when stood down on half pay in 1777 to take ship for America and demand from George Washington the rank of major-general, even though he was only a captain at home, who had never fired a shot in anger during his six years in the service.[8] He took a dozen other officers with him, but they were not so lucky. Washington was known to have cursed all these Frenchmen coming over to offer him their services – as officers of course. Eventually around 100 French noblemen served as volunteers in the Continental Army of the United States. Some, like the Baron de Kalb, were killed in action there. But the ones the Americans found most valuable, fighting as they were against British regulars, were engineers like Jean-Baptiste de Gouvion. As one would expect with a technical branch officer, however, Gouvion was of very recent nobility. He rose to colonel in the American army, but had to wait until 1787 to reach the equivalent rank in France.

And the volunteers were not just confined to unemployed French officers. The numbers of the French were in fact dwarfed by the Poles. Six hundred members of the *Szlachta* fought in America, most of them former members of the Confederation of Bar, whose struggle for 'Golden Freedom' had precipitated the first partition of their country in 1773.[9] They were now looking for other freedoms to fight for. 'I long to die for such a true cause,' declared Kazimierz Pulaski,[10] 'I wish to expire on the bed of glory; I wish to perish at my post.' After rising to the rank of general, he duly did so, at the siege of Savannah in 1779. Again, the most successful Pole was an engineer, Tadeusz Kosciuszko, who would go on in the 1790s to lead the Polish uprising against the third and final partition. Other noble adventurers – from Hungary, from Denmark, from the Baltic shoreline – offered themselves. Perhaps the most successful was the German Baron von Steuben, an out-of-work former captain, of quite dubious noble credentials, in the Prussian service.[11] But, like the French engineers, he had experience and expertise that the Americans lacked – in this case European battlefield drill and combat with bayonets, essential again against British – and Hessian – regulars. He became inspector-general of the infantry, and unlike most of the volunteers never returned to Europe after the war. Now an American general and large landowner, there was nothing to tempt back this genuine soldier of fortune. More authentically aristocratic Swedes, meanwhile, offered their services indirectly, via the French army, as soon as they learnt that France was offering the Americans open armed support. Thus Hans Axel von Fersen and Curt von Stedingk crossed the Atlantic as French officers. All they wanted was to achieve distinction in action. 'The desire to go to America', wrote Stedingk, 'has become so great and fashionable since Lafayette received such a favourable reception from the whole nation, that it can be compared with nothing less than what the Crusaders of old experienced when they made their way to the Holy Land. As far as I am concerned, who sadly enough cannot be reckoned among their number, it is reason and calculation which have determined the matter.'[12]

All told, between 2 and 3,000 European noblemen fought in the American theatre during the War of Independence.[13] Just over 1,000 of them were regular officers in the French army. Around as many more were officers in the navy. When it became clear in 1778 that the king was proposing to send a full scale expeditionary force, there was a wild scramble to get in to the designated regiments and on to the chosen ships which would transport, accompany and support them in action. Nobles of every level were involved, from great courtiers who intrigued and pulled every string available to them to get a posting, down to grizzled career officers who knew they had no chance of rising to high commands, but saw at least the chance of action, glory and perhaps the *croix de Saint Louis* at the end of it all. There is little evidence that many of them held any brief at all for their American allies and the cause they were fighting for. The important point was not so much that the Americans should win, as that the British should be defeated and humiliated. Even Lafayette who trumpeted his love for liberty and all things American, returned from America in 1779 when it looked as if he might get to take part, as a French officer, in an invasion of England. He only went back west when that prospect faded: but that meant he was at Yorktown, once again in American service, when the British surrendered. And the majority of the troops at Yorktown, though commanded by Washington, were French regulars under the command of Rochambeau; not to mention the fleet that cut Cornwallis off, commanded by de Grasse.

They returned home covered in glory, as they had hoped. Even the naval defeats of the last years of the war could not alter its result. And then, quite unexpectedly, they learnt that their contribution to the achievement of American independence was to be recognised by their former comrades in arms. In December 1783 news arrived in Paris of the formation of a society of former officers in the war.[14] It was to be called the Society of the Cincinnati, named after the Roman hero who had left his farm to save the republic as dictator, and, having done that, laid down his powers before their term to return to the plough. A branch had been set up in each of the 13 states, and French officers were invited to establish a fourteenth. And this new society had two special attractions which noble officers found irresistible. It was to have an insignia – an American bald eagle suspended from a blue ribbon edged with white: blue for America, white for Bourbon France. And it was to be hereditary, passed on by primogeniture down the generations to mark out for ever the families who had contributed to the establishment of American freedom. The qualifications for membership were three years' service in the war at the rank of colonel or above.

Cincinnati medal, reproduced by permission of The Society of the Cincinnati,
Washington, DC

Lafayette and Rochambeau were invited to organise a French branch – Lafayette for the volunteers, Rochambeau for the regulars. They both wrote independently to Vergennes to seek the king's permission, including the right to wear the eagle alongside their French decorations. Traditionally, French officers were not allowed to display foreign decorations, with the sole, very distinguished, exception of the Golden Fleece. But Louis XVI granted their request, a signal mark of royal approval. The French branch was inaugurated at well-publicised ceremonies in Paris in mid-January 1784.

It set off the sort of undignified stampede to which noblemen were all too prone. Everybody who had served in the war wanted to get in, and to show it. 'All that mattered to us', recalled the young Comte de Ségur, son of the war minister, who had been determined to be sent to America and switched regiments in order to do it,[15] 'was the pleasure of showing this warrior's palm on our chests, and to draw the gaze in public places of a crowd of idlers attracted and assembled by the least novelty.' Lafayette wanted to keep it exclusive, but there were endless complaints from those who felt excluded: from officers who had never made colonel; from officers who had served in the war but not on the American mainland; from others who had served, but for less than three years; from some who had only vaguely heard about it, but wanted to display 'the cross of Saint Signatus'.[16]

And what about naval officers? The American founders of the society had offered membership to four French admirals, but nobody else. This was surely some sort of mistake, complained the Count d'Estaing, the senior admiral who had served in the war. His former captains were 'mortified' at their exclusion. Their claims were duly admitted, but by August 1784 the king and his ministers were becoming alarmed at the expansion of the society, and permission to add new members was suspended. But it was now firmly established, and had in fact admitted its first hereditary member, the son of Baron de Kalb, who had been killed at Camden in 1780. A new, international order of chivalry had been created. Among its other European members were Kosciuzko and the two Swedes, Fersen and Stedingk – even though they had to struggle with their own monarch Gustav III to wear their eagles, which he considered an unwelcome badge of defiance against kings.[17]

Established the Society may have been, but clearly it was a rich source of strife and bad blood among noblemen instinctively inclined to seek distinctions and feel affronted if they did not receive them. One excluded officer even travelled to America to seek admission from Washington himself, declaring that 'Disappointment would be a stain upon my honour, which could never be blotted out.'[18] And by this time news had arrived that the new society was in trouble in the United States itself. Within months of its foundation, in May 1783, in fact, the Society of the Cincinnati found itself denounced as un-American and un-republican, an attempt to set up that alien European thing, a hereditary nobility. First announced at General von Steuben's headquarters as the victorious army was disbanding, it was widely believed to have been introduced by him to ape the orders of chivalry of Germany. The first idea for such a society had in fact come not from Steuben, but from General Henry Knox, who had been a Boston bookseller before the war, but had come to love the parades and display of military life. But that scarcely mattered. In the perception of Judge Aedanus Burke of South Carolina, a Catholic immigrant from Ireland, the Cincinnati were the germ of a hereditary American peerage. Writing under the eminently republican *nom de plume* of Cassius, in *Considerations on the Society or Order of the Cincinnati*, Burke declared that the new society was dangerously un-republican, if not positively against the provision in the Articles of Confederation which prohibited nobility. He called it 'a dangerous insult to the rights and liberties of the people, and a fatal stab to that principle of equality, which forms the basis of our government'.

Burke's pamphlet, widely disseminated and re-printed in the American press,[19] triggered off the first of many postwar debates about what sort of society the United States was to be. There was huge controversy over the winter of 1783–84. It particularly alarmed George Washington, who had agreed to be the new society's president-general, and as such was due to preside its first plenary meeting scheduled for May 1784. He quickly discerned that the key issue was heredity. So long as membership of a closed society of eminent men was to pass down the generations, the Cincinnati looked like the sort of caste that the nobilities of Europe were taken to be. And since this was the first interstate civilian body to be established in the United States of America, with its own military traditions and its own funds (one of the original ideas of the founders) there was no wonder it looked dangerous for the future of the whole republic. Washington did not believe it was, but he also believed in the supreme importance of appearances, and appearing to be above suspicion. By the time of the general meeting he had come to believe that its establishment had been a mistake, and he appears to have arrived at the meeting intending to recommend that the Society dissolve itself. But at this very moment news arrived from France of the establishment of the branch there, with the full consent of Louis XVI. The emissary who brought this news (Major L'Enfant, later the planner of Washington DC) also brought a consignment of eagle insignia made in Paris, including one encrusted with diamonds for the president-general to wear, donated by officers of the French navy. In these circumstances the general did not feel he could call explicitly for the disbandment of the Society. All he could do was demand the renunciation of heredity. It was no easy struggle, and only by threatening to resign did he win acceptance for the principle. Even then it was not made binding on all the state branches; and as noted earlier the French branch had already admitted its first hereditary member. Several state societies refused to accept this recommendation, in fact; but Washington's action did have the effect of largely snuffing out the American controversy; even though the success of the Society in France had prevented him from securing the entire dissolution of the offending organisation.[20] Later – we should note – even those state societies which renounced heredity reinstated it, and a hereditary Society of the Cincinnati exists to this day, with magnificent headquarters in Washington, DC. It has never become an American nobility or peerage, as Aedanus Burke feared, although it is of course by nature an exclusive caste. But we can fairly say that it owes its survival of the traumas of its birth to the eager way in which French noblemen flocked to join it and display its insignia.

But if the abandonment of heredity defused opposition to the Cincinnati in America, the effects of the controversy were far from over. In fact, a determined effort was now made to bring it to the attention of Europe. The idea came from none other than Benjamin Franklin. Franklin was long on record, since his days as a journalist in the 1720s, as scorning all ideas of hereditary distinction.[21] This did not stop him mingling with the cream of French aristocratic society, with evident pleasure, during his years as United States plenipotentiary in Paris between 1777 and 1784. But when he heard of the controversy in America in January 1784 he was scathing about the new society and its eagle emblem. A turkey, he said, in a private letter to his daughter, would be a more authentically American bird.[22] And leaving aside the dubious constitutionality of the new society under the Articles of Confederation, the hereditary principle rekindled all his old contempt for ancestral claims. Mathematically, he argued, after nine generations only 1/512 of an original ancestor's blood would be left in a descendant's veins. He was so pleased with this letter, in fact, that he considered printing it on his own private press and having it distributed in France. It took his philosophic friend the Abbé Morellet to dissuade him from such an undiplomatic course. He then had another idea: he could perhaps get somebody to

Mirabeau by Jean-Antoine Houdon

publish a French translation of Aedanus Burke's great tract against the Cincinnati. The person he found was Mirabeau, a notorious renegade nobleman in need of a source of income and an occupation to distract him from his debts and sexual scandals in which he was involved. He also made contact with the playwright Chamfort, whose English was better than Mirabeau's, and who, in his rather scanty writings, had a track record of criticising noblemen – even though he lived largely on handouts from the courtier Count de Vaudreuil. Together they produced, by July 1784, a free adaptation of Burke's pamphlet, which Mirabeau published in his own titled name, the Count de Mirabeau, from England in the autumn.

Franklin described it as a 'covered satire against noblesse in general'. It was in fact much more of an open attack. Although it discussed the Cincinnati at length, and lucubrated over Washington's involvement with the Society, it spent most of its text rehearsing general arguments against all claims to hereditary distinction. Nobility was un-republican – that went without saying. But it was also against the human equality enshrined in nature. Turning on its head a favourite myth of noble origins in heroic conquest, Mirabeau argued that present day nobles were descended from barbarian marauders, robbers and assassins, or, more recently, plunderers of the public purse who had used their ill-gotten gains to buy offices. However honourably bestowed on the founder of a dynasty, there was no guarantee that any of his good qualities would pass to his descendants. Nobility was merely a matter of vanity, or simply opinion, harmful as much to those who enjoyed or claimed it, as to the society they lived in 'because they find it more convenient to enjoy a conventional, than to deserve a personal dignity; because it renders them haughty and indolent; because it leaves them no prospect of advancement, but in the trade of a soldier, which requires neither abilities nor industry; because it founds upon hereditary pride an inequality of fortune, which is as prejudicial to particular families, as it is to the state.

Such is the perennial source of vanity and beggary, of meanness and pride, of slavery and tyranny, which pours over countries infected with this lineal nobility all kinds of public and private evils.'[23] From Franklin Mirabeau took the calculation of thinning blood down the generations, and also the observation that to ennoble ancestors, like the Chinese, was a much better way of acknowledging merit than passing on titles to descendants. For good measure, Mirabeau added the text of Richard Price's *Observations on the Importance of the American Revolution*, which had just been published when he arrived in England in search of a printer. The advice which the radical Welsh Unitarian offered to the newly independent American republic was to avoid granting any hereditary honours and titles, and to get rid of primogeniture.

The impact made by this great polemic, it has to be said, was muted. News of its publication soon reached France – another scandalous publication by that notorious rake, who signed himself the *Count* de Mirabeau even as he denounced the pretensions of his own order, and of a society of which his own brother (who had fought in America) was a member. But, printed in England, copies were hard to find in Paris, and only became readily available early in the summer of 1785. Eventually it was translated into English, Dutch and German.[24] By then, however, American issues were old news, and public opinion in France was transfixed by other sensations, including the Mesmerist controversy and the Diamond Necklace affair. Nevertheless, Mirabeau's *Considerations on the Order of Cincinnatus* was a landmark. It was the first open and unequivocal attack on the principle of nobility ever published; and appeared only five years before the French National Assembly attempted to abolish nobility altogether in June 1790. In this way the attitude of the American revolutionaries towards nobility and all that it involved fed directly into the intellectual atmosphere in which the *French* Revolution broke out – with its own profoundly anti-aristocratic character.

Attacks on certain aspects of the nobility, and noble behaviour, were of course nothing new.[25] By scouring the literature of the eighteenth century, and indeed the classical literature, ancient and modern, with which eighteenth-century men were familiar, one can find plenty of hostility. Readers of Dante, of Machiavelli (like the American colonists, as mentioned earlier), of More, of Cervantes, of Molière or La Bruyère could find plenty of denunciations of almost any of the ways in which nobles behaved. The inadequacies of noble values were also exposed in mid-century French discussions of how the kingdom's economic and military performance could be improved. The most familiar is, I suppose, the quarrel over the Abbé Coyer's tract *La Noblesse commerçante*, provoking the Chevalier d'Arc's vigorous riposte *La Noblesse militaire*.[26] There were also hand-wringings about the damage nobility did, from writers like d'Argenson and d'Holbach. And everybody has heard, of course, of *The Marriage of Figaro*, first performed at the very moment when the controversy over the Cincinnati was at its height across the Atlantic, with its feckless and lascivious noble villain, denounced in a celebrated last-act speech by the eponymous hero. But the nobles who engineered the play's presentation in the teeth of royal disapproval, and flocked to see it, no more felt threatened by it than by the glancing blows coming from all those other well-known writers.[27] None of this hostility was focused or sustained. Many of the attacks were aimed at reforming the nobility rather than denouncing it root and branch, at making it more worthy of its destiny rather than denying that destiny altogether.

But the American revolutionaries had done just that, claiming that nobility was both useless and dangerous. The Cincinnati controversy reinforced that message, and the society acknowledged it in renouncing heredity. (A decision, incidentally, which the French branch accepted, and implemented: when de Grasse, the commanding admiral at Yorktown, died in 1788, his son had a request for admission on grounds of heredity turned down.) Franklin, Mirabeau and Chamfort passed on the essence of the American attitude in producing their adaptation and amplification of Burke's pamphlet. Europeans now knew that other Europeans beyond the seas had decided quite consciously to live without hereditary elites. All the well-worn and traditional arguments against hereditary distinctions could now be rehearsed, as Mirabeau rehearsed them, in the knowledge that they were not just theoretical, but could sustain social reality. Many of these arguments resurfaced, with violent force, in the autumn of 1788 in debates over the composition of the Estates-General – debates which ensured that the French Revolution would be anti-noble, anti-aristocratic (to use its own terminology) right from the start. And Franklin's original letter to his daughter of 1784, cannibalised by Mirabeau, was first integrally printed in June 1790, in the *Journal of the Society of 1789*, to defend the National Assembly's decision to abolish the French nobility altogether.[28] Franklin was in everybody's mind just then: only a few days before, news of his death had been announced to the Assembly – in a dramatic intervention by Mirabeau. Mirabeau himself was no longer greatly interested in the issue of nobility. He was not present in the Assembly when it voted the abolition. But Lafayette was there, and so were a number of French Cincinnati. In fact these noblemen took a prominent part in helping to expedite the abolition of their own order. They were the main speakers in the debate of 19 June, these noblemen who had rushed or clamoured to go to America in the 1770s.[29] It has long been recognised that French intervention in America precipitated the French Revolution by the crippling debts which it imposed on the old monarchy. But, insofar as that intervention was planned and carried out by noblemen, brought to triumph by their presence in 1781, and released a full-blown anti-noble ideology in the new republic, spreading from there into Europe, noblemen had been digging their own grave long before the French Revolution pitched them into it.

PART III
NAPOLEON: AN UNDEMOCRATIC REVOLUTIONARY

CHAPTER 10

The Napoleonic Nobility Revisited

In June 1790 the French National Assembly voted to abolish nobility and all its outward signs. Never before in history had a community committed itself to the expurgation of its own hereditary elite. The effect on the nobility of France was traumatic, and the decision sent a warning to its equivalents all over Europe. Yet one of the outstanding facts about the abolition was that it did not work – or at least not in the comprehensive way its authors intended. Nobles could not be prevented from thinking of themselves as noble, from transmitting that conviction to their descendants, or from acknowledging others possessed of the same quality. Public recognition could be denied, but the sense of nobility persisted. Eventually, in 1808, a ruler himself born noble re-created a titled elite, seemingly surrendering to instincts which could not be eradicated. The creation of an imperial nobility has often been depicted, along with the restoration of the altars and the establishment of an imperial monarchy, as one of the great betrayals by Napoleon of the legacy of the Revolution; and perhaps the ultimate one, in the sense that the original revolutionary impulse was profoundly anti-aristocratic. But, like the previous abolition, re-creation raised as many problems as it tried to resolve, both for contemporaries and for historians.

What is often overlooked is that neither Napoleon nor his principal collaborators ever called what he created in 1808 a nobility – at least while he was in power. Not only that. He and they were quite explicit that the purpose of the new creation was to destroy what was left of the old nobility by eclipsing it. 'I instituted the new nobility', he told Dr O'Meara on St. Helena, 'to *écraser* the old.'[1] Napoleon's purpose was also to reward the loyalty of his followers, and to build up a permanent body of support for what he hoped would be the Bonaparte dynasty. To this end he wanted to be the only source of reward and distinction in his empire. The old nobility by contrast owed its identity to pre-existing authorities and traditions over which he had no control. All of them went back to monarchical times, however, and when France had once more become a monarchy in 1804, some nobles had begun to use their titles again and flaunt their coats of arms. The emperor noted this with strong disapproval; and he said that one of the motives for creating the new hierarchy was to stop that trend.[2] It is true that informally and unofficially the new body was often referred to as a nobility, but the first official use of that description came, amazingly enough, from Louis XVIII. It came in the charter of 1814, after Napoleon's downfall. Here the restored Bourbon monarch declared that 'the old nobility will resume its titles, the new will retain its own'.

On this basis, families whose heads had been given titles by Napoleon would find themselves recognised as noble throughout the nineteenth century. After all, they had now been confirmed in the status by the traditionally uncontested source of ennoblement, a legitimate monarch. Nevertheless there was an immediate outcry from the old nobility, and it serves to emphasis that, whatever Napoleon's creation was, it was not a restoration. For it was rapidly pointed out that most families of the old nobility had not possessed titles, whereas all Napoleonic ones did. What the

Emperor had created, in fact, was not so much a nobility as a hierarchy of state servants much closer (as has often been pointed out) to Peter the Great's Russian Table of Ranks of 1722. The actual titles, like Peter's, were borrowed from existing models – princes, dukes, counts, barons, knights – but they were closely tied to functions in the state, whether civil or military. And in principle they were entirely personal. There was no implication that their holders would pass on their status in the blood, as old nobles did, to all their children. Heredity was not indeed entirely ruled out. A title might be transmitted to an eldest son by primogeniture, but only provided that the holder set up a *majorat*, an entailed landed endowment of sufficient value to allow the heir to maintain the status. A *majorat* had to be officially worth a certain sum – 200,000 francs for a prince, 30,000 francs for a count, 15,000 francs for a baron, 3,000 francs for a knight. From a poor noble family himself, Napoleon was convinced that titles and the status that went with them had to be underpinned by appropriate levels of wealth. The insatiable demands to make provision for poor nobles had been one of the constant issues confronting pre-revolutionary governments. Napoleon had himself benefited from such provisions in his youth with his scholarship to a military academy, but he did not want his own regime to be saddled with the problem. So as a general rule, *majorats* had to be applied for, the requisite wealth demonstrated, and only then were they officially approved and registered. Of the 3,600 or so title-holders created between 1808 and 1814, 1,531 were accorded *majorats*.[3] Thus less than half of this Napoleonic aristocracy was in principle hereditary – a fundamental difference from the traditional nobility. On the other hand, when they were confirmed as a nobility by Louis XVIII, all of them immediately adopted the traditional practice of passing on their status to all their children. *Majorats* continued to be granted until the July Monarchy, but now they were seen chiefly as a means of keeping lands together where the Civil Code enjoined equal division between all heirs. Heredity had been definitively detached from them.

In the sense that they conferred exceptions to the common law of the Code, *majorats* were privileges. It is often said that one great difference between Napoleon's title-holders and the old regime nobility was that they enjoyed no privileges, but here is clear evidence that some did. There are other examples: for instance all of them had the exclusive right to display coats of arms – though of new, Napoleonic design. There was a whole hierarchy of precedence governing life at the Emperor's court and access to the sovereign. As time went by, Napoleon said, some members of his new elite would have to be granted privileges to reward further service.[4] But at least there was never any restoration under Napoleon of the vast and bizarre range of advantages enjoyed by nobles in France until 1789. Above all, the new elite enjoyed no tax-exemptions. Quite the reverse: under Napoleon, and throughout the nineteenth century, the elite was defined by how *much* taxation it paid, not how little, and he decorated most of the highest payers with titles.

It might also be countered that if imperial title-holders were a service elite, so was the pre-revolutionary nobility, in the sense that its members officered the king's armed forces and staffed all the higher ranks of the administration and the judiciary. These monopolies were another of the things which the revolutionaries castigated as abuses and sought to overthrow in 1789. But now there were plenty of differences. Before 1789 the king's discretion played very little part in awarding most the offices and ranks in his service. Most of these posts, civil or military, were purchased from previous owners, and royal consent was a mere formality. Purchase also guaranteed tenure, and the king could not dismiss his officers without refunding the capital which they had tied up in their posts. These were not the sort of servants Napoleon wanted. He was scornful of any sort of tenure: it made servants independent of their master, and able to obstruct or defy his will. It is striking that he always resisted the claim of members of his Senate to be made hereditary, however much he heaped them with rewards and honours in other ways. Like many contemporaries, he thought the downfall of the old regime had been brought about largely by the resistance and obstructionism of tenured nobles. And he certainly disapproved of the idea that anybody might buy the right to serve. Military purchase, as well as the sale of civil offices, had been finally abolished by the revolutionaries in the name of careers open to the talents, and the Emperor himself was the very embodiment of this principle. He wanted the members of his governing elite to be the same.

A social analysis of Napoleonic title-holders bears this out.[5] It is true that a quarter of them were members of the old nobility – but this too can be accounted a success if one of the purposes of the new elite was to trump the old one. And 58 per cent of its members came from the bourgeoisie, and almost a fifth (19.5 per cent) from the lower ranks of society. And while it is true that all recent scholarship has tended to show that the old regime nobility was by no means as closed and exclusive as revolutionary myth, and the credulity of too many subsequent historians, suggested, the importance of purchase in its recruitment ensured that it only replenished itself from the top echelons of bourgeois wealth and that nobody ever got in directly from lower down. How men from lowly backgrounds did it under Napoleon, of course, was mostly through the army, in a state geared to almost perpetual warfare. Napoleon had been determined to reward military service spectacularly since even before he became emperor, through the Legion of Honour.

Created in 1802, the Legion is often identified as a direct ancestor of the imperial nobility; and the First Consul found himself having to defend it against the charge that it was a recreation of pre-revolutionary orders of chivalry which nobles had largely monopolised. All republics, he observed, had systems of public reward for outstanding service; and it was in this connection that he made his famous remark that it is by playthings that men are governed.[6] But when the imperial hierarchy of titles was created six years later, all members of the Legion were formally incorporated into it at the lowest grade, that of *chevalier* or knight. One of the most striking features of the early years of the Legion of Honour is the rapid expansion of its numbers. Originally it was intended to comprise not more than 5,000 members, but already by 1805 this number had more than doubled. 1,227 new members were created in 1808 alone, and by the end of that year the Legion was 20,393 strong. It had reached over 38,000 by 1814. Where then does that leave the supposed complement of the imperial hierarchy, generally accepted by historians as somewhere between 3,200 and 3,600?[7] The biggest single category within it, the Knights of the Empire, appear in the standard calculation at around 1,500. Clearly this cannot include the knights of the Legion; so how should we treat them? This is more than a technical question, because on how we answer it depends any estimate of the new aristocracy's weight in society, not to mention any numerical comparison between it and the pre-revolutionary nobility.

Until recently there was no scholarly consensus about how numerous the nobility was in 1789. Respectable estimates ranged between 120,000 and 400,000. But now the careful and cautious estimates of Michel Nassiet[8] suggest that the true figure was around 140,000; so all previous comparative calculations need to be redone. A further complication also seems to have been overlooked by those who have offered such comparisons. The totals from before 1789 comprise all noble *persons*, including women and children. We ought therefore to include in any comparison the families of Napoleonic title holders, even though technically the father's title conferred no special status on his family. That would imply multiplying any totals by something like five. The result, on the narrow estimate of numbers, would give an aristocracy of around 18,000. That would still make its numerical weight in society much less than that of the pre-revolutionary nobility, given that the Empire at its height had about 44 million inhabitants, whereas the kingdom in 1789 had just over 28. If, on the other hand, we include all members of the Legion and their putative families, the total rises to 190,000, which is a much more comparable proportion.

Clearly the Legion skews the whole calculation; and right from the start the Council for the Seal of Titles, a sort of college of heralds set up to adjudicate on all matters relating to titles, pressed the Emperor to deny the title of knight to simple members of the Legion. Knight of the Empire, they said, should be a title restricted to those receiving a specific personal grant by letters-patent rather than automatically on appointment to the Legion.[9] But Napoleon always refused to deny the title of knight to any member of the Legion of Honour, the vast majority of whom were soldiers who had shown all the traditional knightly virtues. Fewer members are soldiers in our own times, but they all still remain technically *chevaliers*. All the Emperor would agree to was to raise the threshold which allowed them to make their titles hereditary by the constitution of a *majorat*. Legionaries would need to have assets worth 3,000 francs, and three subsequent generations would have to demonstrate that they retained this level of wealth before a truly hereditary title would be recognised. But this seems an acknowledgement that knights of the Legion would have access to privileges like the rest of the titled hierarchy, and lends justification to including them in overall totals.

In reality, of course, a provision like this remained entirely notional, in the sense that the six-year existence of Napoleonic titles as originally constituted allowed no time for such drawn-out procedures to take effect. The Emperor himself recognised that it needed time for his new institutions to take root, and looking back from St. Helena he recognised again and again that time was one thing he did not have.[10] The old nobility, by contrast, had time on its side; and if the new hierarchy was inaugurated as a device for eclipsing them, from the start the Emperor also made special efforts to secure recruits from among them in order to give his creation more authentic aristocratic solidity. In the end over 700 of the non-legionary titles, about a quarter of the total, went to men who had been noble before the Revolution. Napoleon would have liked more, but a hard core remained immune to his blandishments, and far more simply did not meet the preconditions of wealth which he thought so essential. Even many of those who qualified for and accepted his titles turned against him in the final crisis of 1814, as the restoration of a legitimate monarch loomed. It was no surprise, therefore, that when Napoleon returned in the Hundred Days he reissued the revolutionary law of 1790 abolishing nobility. He created more titles of his own during that time, but few of these went to old nobles. The new man that he claimed he was during his brief return seems to have given up on the doomed idea of incorporating the old elite into the new.

But, as noted at the beginning, the titled elite created by the usurper survived, and was actually recognised as a nobility by Louis XVIII and all subsequent regimes which recognised noble status at all. Although it took several generations to achieve intermarriage on a significant scale with the old nobility – that ultimate recognition – eventually it happened. And right from the start many old nobles were prepared to accept new ones as junior partners in the perpetuation of noble values. In all these senses Napoleon's attempt to create a new aristocracy was far from a failure; and time and long ancestry, which he himself as a noble of old stock thought essential characteristics for making true nobles, counted for next to nothing when his own creation was recognised by those who succeeded him. It was always largely a myth, assiduously cultivated by nobles everywhere, that authentic nobility is the work of time and the product of a long series of distinguished ancestors. Historically, the most successful nobilities have been the ones with smooth and ample procedures for replenishing themselves with new blood. What finally gave the lie to that myth was the acceptance at one blow by Louis XVIII of the holders of several thousand titles, none more than six years old.

For a fifth of the non-legionary title-holders, of course, it probably mattered little. They were noble anyway under older rules. But for the rest, a large majority however you calculate it, it was a genuine triumph, a consecration of social ascent now recognised *both* by the former regime and the restored one. Here, surely, we can see Napoleon the title-giver as the heir of the Revolution rather than its destroyer or betrayer. For all his attempts to decorate it with some authentic aristocratic tone, in concept Napoleon's aristocracy was essentially meritocratic. If the fundamental social and institutional aspiration of 1789 was careers open to talent, then the Napoleonic aristocracy was the ultimate recognition and institutionalisation of that principle. Or, as the man himself put it: 'I remain with the Revolution, because my nobility is in no way exclusive. My titles are a sort of civic crown; they can be earned through works.'[11] But there is also another side to this. After Napoleon fell, no new imperial titles were created. Newly recognised as a true nobility, his aristocracy became a closed hereditary caste, and merit no longer had anything to do with it. Its destiny was not to perpetuate the meritocratic values through which it was created, but to wither away by genetic attrition, its remnants absorbed into the ranks of what even they recognised as real nobles.[12]

CHAPTER 11

Napoleon, Women and the French Revolution

Everybody knows something about Napoleon. Everybody has a vague idea of who he was, and what he did, and of course what he looked like. He is one of that handful of figures in history who is universally known by his first name only; and perhaps the only one whose portrait everybody instantly recognises. Napoleon said and wrote a lot, and in a crisp, direct style which made what he said and wrote memorable. Even so, nobody except specialists or Napoleon-buffs remembers much of it. But there is one remark of Napoleon that everybody does remember – even though ironically (like Marie-Antoinette's *Let them eat cake*) we have no evidence that he ever did say it. *Not tonight, Josephine.* It is the mainspring of innumerable ribald jokes, and even adverts on television: and the inference it makes about Napoleon is clear. Here was a man of great sexual power and attraction, with a wife who pleaded for his favours and got nowhere. A starting point is to discuss how true a picture this was.

The first problem is to disentangle the man from the ruler, if indeed this is really possible. After all, Napoleon was a ruler for half his adult life, and the commander of victorious armies for four years in addition to that. As Henry Kissinger once said, power is a great aphrodisiac, and during his years of power Napoleon was able to call upon almost any woman he wanted, and there was never any shortage of women prepared to make themselves available to him. The only evidence we have of Napoleon's relationship with women *before* he became a great man and did not have the freedom of choice that gave him, is the case of Desirée Clary. Napoleon said that Desirée was the first woman to attract him. He met her in Marseille in 1793, when he and his whole family had been driven out of Corsica by Corsican separatists. He even made her the heroine of the novel he wrote around the time, *Clisson et Eugénie*. *His* brother Joseph married *her* sister Julie, so she remained part of the family. She did in fact become a queen, but not Napoleon's: in 1798 she married Jean-Baptiste-Jules Bernadotte, whom Napoleon made a marshal and who, in 1818, became king of Sweden. She seems to have been genuinely attracted to Napoleon, but she saw nothing much of him after 1793, and in 1796 he finally cast her aside. By then he had met Josephine.

Desirée seems to have loved him more than he ever loved her. And that was because from only a few months after they met he was much more in love with something else: his own power and glory, and the celebrity life that it gave him. At one level, it could almost be said that the only person Napoleon was ever in love with was himself: he was indeed the complete narcissist, the man who said at one point 'What are a million lives to a man like me?' Such thoughts were far ahead of him in 1794 and 5, but even then that singleminded drive to distinguish himself, seize every opportunity, not get caught in situations with no future, were plainly visible; and we can be certain that with all this he did not give Desirée much thought. And by the time he reached national prominence, in the early autumn of 1795, he already had no more need to spend time looking around for emotional attachments. Women came looking for him, a rising young man with big prospects. And this is where Josephine came in.

She was a penniless widow with two children to support and expensive tastes. She was by all accounts very sexy, and she lived from day to day by offering herself to the rich and powerful, what we would call a gold-digger. But she was also no longer young, at 33, and some said her looks, and particularly her teeth, were deteriorating. Bonaparte might be the last best chance she had, and he *was* the man of the moment. So she encouraged him, as she had encouraged others before him, only to find that she got more than she had bargained for. He fell passionately, violently in love with her, and insisted they marry. An inexperienced but passionate young man was seduced by a very experienced older woman who in turn found his attentions rapidly overwhelming. Luckily for her, she only had to endure them for a few weeks after their marriage in March 1796, when he went off to command the army in Italy – and make his name as a general in the field.

Who knows if that would have been the end of Napoleon's sexual adventures, but for two things. One was Josephine's infidelity. Hardly had he disappeared over the Alps than she was encouraging other lovers, while at the same time luxuriating in the glory of being the wife of the hero of Italy. He kept urging her to come and join him, in a passionate stream of letters, but she put it off as long as she could, and when she did eventually go, she had a young lover with her. Napoleon appears not to have noticed, and it was only when Josephine failed to join him on his expedition to Egypt in 1798, for perfectly good reasons that he could not know (she had been injured in a building collapse) that one of his aides decided that there was enough evidence to tell him what everyone else knew already. The effect was electric. Napoleon vowed to divorce her as soon as he got back to France. Meanwhile he took his revenge by publicly taking a mistress, the wife of one of his junior officers, Pauline Fourès. Apparently he told her that if she gave him a son, he would divorce Josephine and marry her.

And this is the second thing that kept Napoleon's sexuality going. He wanted a son. He had already made this clear to Josephine.

The place where she was injured in 1798 was Plombières, a spa where the waters were supposed to promote conception. But by now she would soon be too old to have children, and then what? On Napoleon's side, there was the creeping fear that he might be infertile. For a red-blooded Corsican, married now for four years, that was humiliating enough; and it is noteworthy that when Pauline Fourès failed to become pregnant, he lost interest in her. Meanwhile it was a humiliation he seemed prepared to live with, and when he returned from Egypt in 1799 it was to take power, back in France. As head of state he felt more dignified with a consort, and it was probably that which saved Josephine from divorce when he did get back; or at least that and the realisation by Josephine herself that she could no longer sail close to the wind. Caesar's wife must be above suspicion, and she abandoned *her* lover. The passion between her and Napoleon was gone, but they now rubbed along, and she behaved well in public, which he seems to have appreciated. But when, in 1804, they became an emperor and empress, the problem resurfaced more urgently. Monarchs need heirs of their body to perpetuate their line, and preferably sons – especially in France, where succession had always been under the Salic Law, and no woman had ever reigned. By this time Napoleon had developed a habit of sleeping with whoever he fancied. Josephine too seems to have believed that he was infertile, and raised no trouble about it. Quick liaisons became his style, snatched in spare moments. There are stories of girls waiting undressed in the freezing cold for hours and then being told to go away because the great man was too busy. In 1806, however, one of these swift liaisons had an unexpected result. Eléonore Denuelle, employed to read to Josephine, was bedded by Napoleon almost as soon as he saw her, and nine months later she had a son. He was called, half after his father, Léon. Apparently he looked like Napoleon, who liked to see him from time to time, and left him substantial sums in his will. The idea even seems to have crossed his mind to legitimise him and make him his heir. But this was never very serious. The importance of Léon was that he showed Napoleon that he *could* have children, and boys at that. From then on Josephine was doomed, even though Napoleon by now seems to have been genuinely fond of her: witness his decision to crown her as well as himself at the imperial coronation, in the teeth of opposition from his entire family. But as time went by he worried more and more about the absence of direct heirs. And then, in 1807, when she was far away, he fell in love for the second time in his life.

This time it was Maria Walewska, a Polish countess whom he met while campaigning in the east against the Russians. He was smitten by her, and as soon as they saw this, the Polish nobles of the circles in which she moved pressed her to offer herself to him. They saw Napoleon as the liberator of their country, wiped off the face of the map in 1795 by the three eastern powers whom Napoleon had defeated or (in the case of Russia) was about to. She was reluctant, but that made Napoleon all the more ardent, and within a few weeks she had succumbed. Napoleon for his part did not find himself thinking of her as just another passing fancy. He kept on seeing her, and eventually, in May 1810, she gave him another son, Alexandre, whom it suited everybody to treat as the legitimate child of her elderly husband. Napoleon saw them both regularly until the eve of his downfall: they visited him on Elba and again before he left Paris after Waterloo to give himself up to the British. Like Léon, he was remembered in Napoleon's will. But the importance of Alexandre Walewski was greater than this. His birth showed once more that Napoleon could have sons. Since shortly after meeting Maria, in fact, having defeated every continental enemy, Napoleon had been thinking seriously about divorcing Josephine; but not to marry his new love, for all their passion. What he wanted was royal links: 'I must be connected with princes', he said. He now wanted not just heirs, but authentic royal heirs. He considered a number of possibilities, but when he defeated the Austrians in a renewed bout of warfare in 1809, the best of all possible solutions, hitherto not available, was opened up. Like so many French rulers before him, he could marry a member of the oldest and most illustrious ruling house in Europe, the Habsburgs. They had little choice, and, defeated as they were, they could see advantages in admitting the Corsican upstart into their family. And so in 1810 it finally happened and (if we discount Henry VIII and Catherine of Aragon), the most famous divorce in history took place; Josephine was cast aside, and Napoleon married the archduchess Marie-Louise. He jumped into bed with her the first night he saw her, and he was delighted by the way she responded. He was even more delighted when, just over a year later, a legitimate son was at last born, the King of Rome. The tragic story of the King of Rome, the eaglet, is well known. After his father's downfall, he grew up to an empty life in Vienna, and died there in 1832 – remembered in France (at least between 1852 and 1870) as Napoleon II, but never ruling anywhere, and showing no obvious affinities with his father's character. But meanwhile his birth marked the end of Napoleon's sexual adventures – or at least any significant ones.

That is the personal record. But Napoleon's attitude to women was more than a personal matter. Napoleon ruled France for 15 years, and intermittently much of Europe during that time. So his views on women and their role were a matter of great importance to half the population at least. Predictably, he had strong views on the matter. His attitude was strictly functionalist: the role of women was to be wives and mothers. Above all, mothers: he once described women as machines for making babies, and on another occasion as fruit-trees to be harvested. At his crudest, he saw them as mere studs for soldiers: another of his famous one-liners was that the losses of a particularly bloody battle could be made up by one night in Paris. But of course the role of women did not end with reproduction. Their function was also to educate and bring up children according to correct principles, and with the right views and attitudes. This was a very heavy responsibility, but one he knew that women could undertake, because that was what they were made for. This conviction came from the example of his own mother, the formidable Letizia, promoted after he became Emperor to the unprecedented title of *Madame Mère*, Madam Mother, the woman who had given the world the wonder-child himself. She seems to have been the only human being whom Napoleon was ever in awe of. She did, after all, have an impressive track-record, widowed at 35 and bringing up eight unruly children, having borne four more who died.[1] She brought them up very strictly, and very religiously, while running a frugal and solvent household after her husband's death. So of all the women in Napoleon's life, she was perhaps the most important of all, an enduring example in his mind of what a woman should be.

She was unrepentantly *un*intellectual. And intellectualism was what Napoleon hated most in women. 'I want', he said in describing his ideal education for girls,[2] '...not women of charm, but women of virtue: they must be attractive because they have high principles and warm hearts, not because they are witty or amusing.' Above all he hated what he called *meddlesome* women, women who interfered in men's affairs, which meant the business of the world. One woman in particular epitomised all that he hated: Mme de Staël.[3] She was the daughter of Necker, Louis XVI's notorious Swiss finance minister who had run up the debts which finally brought down the old monarchy. She grew up attending her mother's *salon* in Paris, the last of the great gatherings of influential hostesses that had played such a part in the propagation of the Enlightenment. This background left her feeling entitled to exercise influence in public affairs. She thought she was important, and deserved to be taken seriously. When Napoleon returned to Paris as the conqueror of Italy in 1797, she tried hard to ingratiate herself with him, and perhaps even hoped to seduce him. He was simply embarrassed, and that rapidly led to annoyance. When, after he took over power, her *salon* and her writings became a centre of opposition to his rule, his first impressions were confirmed. In 1802 she was banished from Paris, and everything she wrote after that was banned wherever Napoleon's writ ran. He considered her both silly and dangerous, and would fly into rages whenever she was mentioned. She was indeed one of the main epicentres of opposition to Napoleonic rule – although this opposition was never more than intellectual and critical. But as such she was a constant irritant to a man who could not stand criticism; and a constant reminder of how appalling women could be if they once tried to go beyond the role that he thought nature had assigned to them.

All this suggests that in reality, behind the appearances, Napoleon was rather afraid of women; or at least the ones he could not control. That was the secret of his mother's power, of Staël's, and perhaps of Josephine's too before he became the ruler of France and not simply her husband. He could not fully control any of them. He had before him too the example of what the ordinary women of Paris had done during the Revolution – dragging the royal family back to Paris in October 1789, pushing their menfolk to violent extremes in August 1792 (when he had been there himself to witness the massacres and the mutilations of male corpses when the monarchy was overthrown), a force pushing both revolution and *counter*-revolution in violent directions when they got the chance. Women in his view had weak minds, and were deeply unstable in their inclinations. They needed to have

constancy inculcated into them. That meant prescribing what
sort of education they should have – or rather, lack of education.
Women, in Napoleon's view, did not need book-learning. What
they should learn was the domestic arts: child-rearing, of course,
but also sewing, dressmaking and so on. 'The advantage of all
this', he said,[4] 'is that they are given practice in everything they
are likely to be called upon to do, and that their time is normally
filled up with sensible and useful occupations.' There was some
advantage in teaching them some mathematics, so that they could
keep household accounts, but none in teaching them languages –
literature would only disturb them. And whereas some science
might be acceptable, the danger was that it might make them
think critically about religion – and that would be fatal. 'Religion',
he said,[5] 'is all important...for girls. Whatever people may say, it
is the mother's surest safeguard, and the husband's. What we ask
of education is not that girls should think, but that they should
believe.' It is well known that Napoleon thought the mysteries of
religion were no more than the mystery of the social order, and that
it was the real key to social control; but clearly he saw the religion
of women as the very mainspring of this. Religious women, just
like his mother, would pass on their religion to their children, thus
ensuring the perpetuity of social order and subordination.

But in case religion was not enough to keep women in their
place, there was also the law. Napoleon declared (however dis-
ingenuously) that while Waterloo would eclipse the memory of
all his previous victories, his code of laws would make his name
live for ever. But for women that code of laws was little more than
a charter of subordination. The ideal behind the Civil Code for
women was for them to pass directly from the tutelage of their
father to that of their husband. If they did not marry, and if they
had some property to support themselves, women might enjoy a
certain independence under the Code. They had an equal right

with male children to a share of parental property, but of course not until parents died; so that many unmarried women would remain in effect dependent even after reaching the age of majority. But once married they had no control over their own property, could do nothing legal without their husband's consent, and could not even bear witness in a court of law. Divorce was possible, as it had been since 1792, but on very unequal terms. A woman could seek divorce only on grounds of her husband's adultery under the conjugal roof; but a man could do so for adultery committed anywhere,[6] for not having children, or even for being too old for children – as with Josephine. Domestic violence against women was almost impossible to prosecute, as was rape; and there was no legal way to establish paternity or paternal responsibility in cases of illegitimacy. Napoleon's world, in short, was a man's world, and women were there for the service of men – their pleasure, their comfort, their reproduction. The only positive thing, it might be argued, that his regime ever did for women was to try to make some state provision for obstetrics and midwifery, to reduce mortality in childbirth.[7] But even this was severely utilitarian in its inspiration. At a time when the French birth rate was beginning to fall, Napoleon was anxious that his reserves of men should not diminish, and safer childbirth was obviously one way of promoting this – good servicing for the baby machines...

All this has long been depicted as a terrible and disappointing step backwards for women, after the emancipatory promise of the French Revolution. And it has been put into the scales in the most time-honoured and endlessly-rehearsed question about Napoleon, the subject of innumerable examination questions still: was Napoleon the perpetuator or destroyer of the work of the French Revolution? The evidence on women has always been thrown in on the negative side, perhaps understandably enough. But how justified is this? And if it is not, then what are the consequences for our understanding of Napoleon's relationship with the Revolution?

Over the last generation interest in the whole question of women and the French Revolution has revived dramatically.[8] Feminist writers – and most others have followed them in this – have argued that, so far from having an emancipatory effect on women, the French Revolutionary project was a deliberate attempt to force women back into an exclusively domestic role. The men of the Revolution believed that women in public life were trouble-makers. The corruption of the old regime monarchy could largely be attributed to the influence of bad women over weak kings. There were the notorious mistresses of Louis XV, including Mme de Pompadour who got France into a disastrous alliance with Austria, and then the trollop Mme Dubarry who helped the king ride roughshod over French law and liberties at the end of his reign. Louis XVI had no mistresses, but he was married to the feckless, extravagant and interfering Marie-Antoinette, the hated *Austrian Woman*, who in addition to being the symbol of the disastrous Austrian alliance, had poured her favours on a string of voracious female favourites. Looking abroad, there was Catherine the Great, the Russian despot, widely believed to have murdered her husband to seize the throne, and who gratified her innumerable lovers with gifts of thousands of helpless serfs. She did this while corresponding with French philosophers: but that was entirely characteristic, too. The Enlightenment itself was shot through by the influence of scheming and ambitious women, *salon* hostesses who enjoyed manipulating influential people.[9] The only philosopher who spurned this world was Jean-Jacques Rousseau, who declared that a woman's place was in the home. Rousseau in turn was much influenced by ancient models of civic virtue, Sparta or Rome, where the men went off to fight and the women stayed behind.

All this came together, gender historians have argued, as part of the revolutionary rejection of the old regime and its corrupt ways. Rousseau was the hero and prophet for the revolutionaries, and in establishing a new world of civic virtue they deliberately set out to exclude women from the public sphere. Never mind the women who brought the king to Paris, or those bizarre revolutionary amazons like Olympe de Gouges who proclaimed women's rights and strutted about in tricolour sashes and caps of liberty: these were all women out of place, like Dr Johnson's dog walking on its hind legs. Even when they achieved something beneficial, it was regrettable that it could not have been achieved some other way, some more ordered way. And later on, when the revolutionaries fell out with the church, women proved to be the mainstay of *counter-revolution*, keeping religion going throughout the time when the revolutionaries were trying to stamp it out.[10] All in all, women were seen as nothing but trouble: and a tremendous quantity of ink has been spilt on what has come to figure as the key moment in the gender history of the Revolution, the suppression in October 1793 of the Society of Revolutionary Republican Citizenesses, a female political club.[11] It was done amid much proclamation that a woman's place was in the home, bringing up babies and ministering to the creature comforts of rugged male patriots.

Now this is quite a powerful case. What, after all, can we think that women actually gained from the Revolution? Not the vote, certainly. Not the right to be elected to anything. Not in the end, as we have seen, the right to any public role at all. The only gain that seems undeniable is easier divorce. By the law of 20 September 1792 divorce was allowed by mutual consent on a wide range of grounds, including incompatibility. Either side could institute proceedings in complete equality, and some women feared that that would allow men to throw off their wives simply because they had grown old. But at least this was a thoroughly equal law, compared to which the Napoleonic provisions in the Code of 1804 were a huge step backwards for women.

Yet note the date of the 1792 law: 20 September. It was therefore passed on the last day of the Legislative Assembly, a body dominated by the Girondins. The Convention, which met the next day, would be dominated by the Montagnards. There appear, in fact, to have been two distinct French revolutionary attitudes to women. The Girondins were actually quite favourable to female equality. Condorcet campaigned for it, and one of the things that held them together was the influence of the *salon* of Mme Roland, the most famous revolutionary woman of all. The most prominent of the revolutionary 'Amazons', Olympe de Gouges and Théroigne de Méricourt, were Girondin supporters. Against them were the Montagnards, who were clearly scared of female power, conciliated the women of Paris only because they saw little alternative, but struck down the women's political clubs as soon as they felt they safely could. It was not 'the Revolution' as some monolithic entity, that was hostile to women and their aspirations. It was the Montagnards, who took over the Jacobin Club and the course of 1793, and drove more liberal and adventurous elements out. It has long seemed to me that the true French revolutionaries were not the Jacobins who gave France terror, but the Girondins who resisted terror and eventually perished by it – not because, as is usually claimed, they were too moderate, but actually because they were too radical.[12] Their more favourable attitude to women certainly seems to fit in with this.

Now in 1792–93, when the differences between Girondins and Jacobins were coming to a head, Napoleon was still a nobody: although one of the few things we know he said in his years of obscurity was to condemn the mobs which assailed the monarchy in 1792, in which women played such a prominent part.[13] But notoriously, Napoleon's first appearance on the national stage came towards the end of 1793, when he was instrumental in recapturing the naval port of Toulon from British occupation. Once that was done, he played his part in shooting the French collaborators whom the British had left behind. He was therefore a terrorist, an instrument of the Jacobin Convention; and he owed the early boosts in his career to links with the brother of Robespierre. When Robespierre fell in July 1794, Napoleon was briefly imprisoned as a suspected creature of the fallen tyrant. And when, in his first command, he mowed down the Vendémiaire insurgents in October 1795 with Carlyle's famous 'whiff of grapeshot', he was at the spearhead of a Jacobin reaction against royalists. Right up until 1799, in fact, Napoleon could plausibly be depicted as a Jacobin, ruthless and destructive. It was only his need to find a scapegoat for his seizure of power in 1799 that made him strike anti-Jacobin poses and depict himself as France's saviour from a return to terror.

If, then, Jacobinism was the real anti-female strain in the Revolution; and if Napoleon is most plausibly identifiable as a Jacobin throughout his early career, then his attitude to women should not seem in the least surprising. It was a thoroughly Jacobin one: against all female meddling in public affairs (although very careful to meet the concerns of the market women of Paris through strict controls over the price of bread), and determined to ensure that women stayed at home under the complete domination of their menfolk. Napoleon's policies on women, so far from reversing what the Jacobin Republic had done for or to them, largely endorsed it.

Whether that was truly revolutionary or not is a rather different question – especially if we accept that the defeated Girondins were in fact more revolutionary than the victorious Jacobins. Either way, Napoleon's divorce legislation represented a final defeat for any Girondin vision of female rights and family life. On the other hand, we have to ask where Napoleon's insistence on women as a vehicle for religious instruction fits in, when one source of Jacobin misogyny was the strength which counter-revolution derived from female religiosity. To emphasise the value of female religiosity hardly seems very Jacobin. And yet, even the Jacobins of 1793 and 1794 did not really blame the women for the so-called 'superstition' and 'fanaticism' which they displayed. They were simply weak and impressionable creatures misled by the wiles of priestcraft. The priests were the problem, not the women. Napoleon thought the same: but, with his unerring realism, he saw that the way to deal with this problem was not to fight its source, but to take it over. Do a deal with the priests, and the problem of women would take care of itself. And that is what happened. By making an agreement with Rome, the Concordat of 1801, Napoleon made the Catholic Church in France an ally rather than an enemy, while ensuring at the same time that he and his agents controlled the French clergy completely. Controlling them, he could control the women, and channel their religiosity into upholding the new order, rather than obstructing it. But they were still the same weak-brained, credulous creatures that the men of 1793 had found so exasperating. The essence of Napoleonic social policy was to turn these weaknesses into strengths for the regime: but let the men (including the priests) get on with running a man's world in the exclusive interests of men.

Napoleon as emperor in uniform, by Jean-Antoine Houdon

CHAPTER 12

The Political Culture
of the French Empire

A quarter of a century ago, in Chicago, there began a great series of conferences which sooner or later brought together most of the leading historians working on the French Revolution around the time of its bicentenary. The theme of these conferences, whose published proceedings eventually stretched to four handsome and weighty volumes, was *The French Revolution and the Creation of Modern Political Culture*.[1] This series was consciously intended by the editors who planned it as a manifesto for a new era in French Revolutionary studies; an era when the Revolution would be studied no longer in terms of class conflict and social movements, but in terms of culture. And in order to set the scene, one of the editors felt obliged at the start of the first volume to offer a definition of what political culture was. 'If politics', wrote Keith Baker,[2] '... is the activity through which individuals and groups in any society articulate, negotiate, implement, and enforce the competing claims they make one upon another, then political culture may be understood as the set of discourses and practices characterizing that activity in any given community.' Political culture, therefore, is our way of conducting public affairs, how we order our governance. And in this context, the great drama of the French Revolution was its attempt to reformulate French ways of governance from scratch, and comprehensively. Sooner or later, every facet of the old political order and the habits by which it worked was renounced. Entirely new rationales for authority, structures to give them working substance, and behavioural expectations to make them work, were all introduced. An absolute monarchy constrained only by custom was to be supplanted by a representative regime – first a monarchy, then a republic – circumscribed by abstractly-defined national and citizens' rights set down in a written constitution. Nothing so all-embracing had ever been attempted before in the history of the world; but the attempt, or something like it, has often been made since. And that is the sense in which those volumes really were about the *creation* of modern political culture.

And yet, within a handful of years, this bold attempt to create brand new contours and habits for political life, untainted by all previous practices, was widely perceived to have failed. Successive attempts to embody a new regime had proved incapable of functioning in a stable and orderly manner. The country had been plunged into chaos, degenerating into a civil war only resolved by the systematic massacre of the Terror and its vengeful aftermath. And this was an experience that nobody felt sure might not be repeated at any moment. Napoleon rode to power on these fears. He set about healing the wounds opened up by the Revolution in masterful and imaginative style. He was young, he had a successful army to back up his authority, and plenty of able collaborators willing him to succeed. But he was not immortal; and the fear was, as his formula for restoring order seemed to be working, that it could all be destroyed if his guiding hand was removed. Over the five years of the Consulate, there were a number of plots aiming to achieve that removal by force. Making the general Consul for life did nothing to solve this problem of continuity, either in the long or short term. The Empire was originally conceived as an answer to this problem.

In a certain sense, therefore, the Empire was itself a product of revolutionary political culture, because it was a *created* regime, the product of a conviction that even an empire could be started from scratch as an act of political will. Nothing could have been more different from the organically evolved thousand-year-old German *Reich*. And, although its central point was to make the ruler of France hereditary, there was never any question of making Napoleon simply king. Partly that was because he wanted to lay down a deliberate challenge to the ruler in Vienna who had hitherto always been *the* Emperor; but probably more importantly it was to emphasise that this new regime was to be in no sense a restoration of traditional French monarchy. For not only might that give the Bourbons the delusion (as it then seemed) that they might one day return to take over a state that they and many others thought legitimately theirs to rule over; it would also disappoint and affront anybody who believed something worthwhile had been achieved by the revolution which had thrown them out. This lay behind the odd formula in the plebiscitary question which gave the change to an empire its veneer of popular legitimacy. It asked for consent for the government of the *republic* to be confided to an emperor.

And a French Empire really was something new. There was no precedent. Although the king of France had ruled various overseas dominions since the sixteenth century, they had never been described as an empire in constitutional terms. And although the term 'French Empire' had been used in the eighteenth century, it was a technical usage akin to that of Henry VIII when, in breaking with the papacy, he described the realm of England as an empire: that is, a jurisdiction acknowledging no superior. Louis XIV, in his less guarded moments, had sometimes fantasised about being elected Holy Roman Emperor, but he must have known that this was really an empty dream. So the only possible precedent for a French Empire had to be sought as far back as Charlemagne, and the problem with that was that the Holy Roman Emperor in Vienna had prior claims on the legacy.

That did not stop Napoleon trying to appropriate the legacy, or at least to trump it. He often declared in so many words, especially in speaking of his relations with the pope, that he was a new Charlemagne.[3] He imitated Charlemagne in having himself crowned king of Italy with the iron crown of the Lombards.[4] The imperial coronation, too, was full of Carolingian echoes and imitations.[5] Appropriately, linking the new empire to Charlemagne also had the advantage of upstaging the family who had eventually usurped Carolingian authority, the Capets. On the other hand, any sort of empire provided useful precedents, especially the greatest and most long-lived of all empires, which all educated men were familiar with, the empire of Rome. Napoleon even had the advantage of looking rather like the known images of the first man who had turned a chaotic republic into a serene empire, Augustus; and his visual propagandists in sculpture made the most of that.[6] Like Augustus, he had no son, and at this stage, given Josephine's age, no likelihood of having one. But Augustus' chief claim to legitimate authority was that he was the adoptive son of Caesar, and the imperial constitution made clear that Napoleon's heir, too, might be an adoptive son.[7]

And there was no provision, either in Napoleon's line or that of the others placed in the line of succession, for women. Why not? It was not simply a matter of Napoleon's notorious personal hostility to women in any sort of position of power. Much more important, surely, was that the Salic law, under which the throne in France had always been inherited, excluded women from succeeding to the crown. Now of course no post-revolutionary regime felt bound in any way by the Salic or any other pre-revolutionary law. But this went deeper than law. This was a matter of habit and instinctive reactions, simply the French way of doing things, a politico-cultural reflex. And the exclusion of women was a particularly vivid example of how, despite 15 years of conscious attempts to uproot the tyranny of habit and custom and to replace it with a political culture planned on lines of utility and rationality, in many ways the political culture of the Empire, new and unprecedented entity though it was, was moulded by instincts deeply embedded within the French body politic and the minds of the men who ran it, ways of ordering and conducting the country's public life as rooted in their way as the well-worn practices of the venerable *Reich* which France's ruler was about to shatter.

From the moment the First Consul broached the idea with him in March 1804, his consular colleague Cambacérès understood exactly what was going on. 'I see', he told Napoleon, 'that everything is taking us back to the former order of things.'[8] And as soon as he left he turned to the other consul, Lebrun, and said, 'The consulate is finished. Imperial monarchy is about to begin.' And, just because it was a *French* imperial monarchy, it was instinctively constructed in the light of French traditions. That is not to say that Napoleon and his advisers set out consciously and deliberately to replicate the ways of the old regime monarchy in every detail. But what they did do was use French history and traditions as a sort of basic template, with Napoleon in effect saying, 'I am now a French monarch. How did previous monarchs in this country do it? How did they conduct themselves? What sort of behaviour and apparatus did they require to make their rule work?' And only then, 'Is there any reason why I should *not* do the same?' That process began at once with the question of a coronation. Should there be one? Yes, all monarchs had one. Coronation did not confer legitimacy, but it was the most important way of flaunting it. So out came all the accounts of previous coronations with the Emperor and his advisers as it were ticking the yes or no boxes on every line. Reims? No. Paris was now the centre of everything, and this was something to be emphasised, not disguised. Regalia? Essential to any monarchical display. But no fleur de lys! This symbol was far too closely associated with the deposed former dynasty. Much preferable were imperial eagles, the fierce and stately emblem deployed by both the Austrian and Russian emperors; and bees, the oldest known symbol of French royalty, far predating the Capets.[9] A solemn oath? Certainly, but not the jumble of ill-assorted commitments made by pre-revolutionary monarchs; instead, a brief brand-new pledge in which the Emperor bound himself to uphold the key revolutionary achievements which he had so far prospered by protecting. Blessing of the church? Of course, a coronation is a religious service. Get the pope himself, who owes the Emperor so much! But Napoleon I, the founder of a dynasty whose very title presumed that he would be succeeded by others of the same name, would not be crowned by the pontiff, or any priest. He owed his crown to his own efforts, and the vague approbation of his people. The box-ticking went on right down to the minutest details of ceremonial. The guiding principle was to follow French precedents unless they appeared to contradict the basic tenets of the new Empire.

Napoleon was a great admirer of the old monarchy and its ways, and he seems to have admired it more as time went by. The only king of France for whom he seems to have had any time at all was Louis XIV,[10] but he saw the institution as far stronger than the individuals who had worn the crown. And he also knew that this mighty and impressive edifice had crumbled, and as its conscious successor he wanted to make sure the same thing did not happen to what he was now involved in setting up for himself and his posterity. Accordingly his whole policy was to replicate those aspects of the old regime which he saw as strengths, and to avoid what he identified as sources of fatal weakness.

These reflexes, it is true, established themselves before the Empire came into being. Napoleon learnt them in his negotiations to restore the altars. This involved giving back the consolations of religion to the French people, and so making the church and its adherents a source of support rather than opposition to established authority in France. But none of it implied bringing back the proud old Gallican church. Its long-confiscated landed wealth was not restored, nor the useless monasteries which had sat on so much of it. Above all, the church's political and institutional independence, as manifested by tax-exemption and quinquennial assemblies of the clergy, made no reappearance. The French church must never again be in a position to hold the country's government to ransom. To achieve this, it is true, the First Consul had to recognise increased spiritual powers for the pope, and as Emperor he was later compelled to deal with some of the unforeseen consequences. Nevertheless the strategy he later adopted towards an unexpectedly obdurate papacy came straight out of French traditions: consciously looking back to Louis XIV, Napoleon reintroduced the four Gallican articles of 1682, and later called what he hoped would be a tame council of bishops to rebut the pretensions of Rome. Taking the pope prisoner so as to bully him in person, was, it is true, something that even Louis XIV had been unable to do, and might well have baulked at if he had. But what Napoleon liked about this great predecessor was his unwillingness to be dictated to, whether by foreigners (including the pope) or *a fortiori* by his own subjects.

Apart from the amazing energy of Napoleon himself, the powerhouse of Napoleonic government was the Council of State. It, too, predated the Empire, coming into being with the Consulate itself. But it was plainly modelled on the pre-revolutionary institution of the same name and it fulfilled similar functions as an administrative and judicial clearing-house, and a place where laws were drafted and refined. Unlike pre-revolutionary kings, the First Consul was often present at the Council of State's deliberations, but once he had become Emperor he was often away on campaign, and then instinct and tradition resurfaced, and the Council largely ran the Empire from day to day without much reference to its master. By then, too, it had also acquired the two-tier character of its old regime namesake, with a complement of virtually tenured councillors of state, serviced by a corps of aspirants called auditors. Before 1789 officials at this level were called masters of requests, and in 1806 an upper rank was introduced going by this very name. They were expected to be men of proven ability, with the potential to prove it yet further, but they were also chosen from men of substantial private means. All that distinguished them from their old order equivalents was that the latter had bought or inherited, and either way owned, their offices.

The venal instinct runs deep in France. One of the more remarkable though relatively unsung achievements of the revolutionaries was to uproot most of the sale of offices, but their hopes of extirpating it entirely were never fully realised. Napoleon allowed the exchange of certain offices for money to re-establish itself among various categories of lawyer.[11] But where it had been at its most spectacular he never considered bringing back sale, because in the courts of law from the sixteenth century right down to the Revolution venality had underpinned tenure, and made it virtually impossible to discipline magistrates who resisted the royal will without reimbursing the moneys that they or their ancestors had paid out. The Emperor Napoleon liked a lot about the old parlements.[12] He created a series of courts of appeal with districts of jurisdiction not unlike the old *ressorts*. He also sought to recruit on to their benches as many of the former parlementaires as he could find, provided they were in easy circumstances. He was closely advised in all this by Lebrun, formerly secretary to Chancellor Maupeou, who had for a time broken the parlements' power during the last years of Louis XV. But as such, Lebrun had been involved in an attempt to abolish judicial venality, and he made sure it was not revived now, any more than were the rights of registration and remonstrance which had enabled the magistrates to obstruct the royal will. There would be no judicial independence, and nothing to make it possible, under the Empire. Just as under Maupeou, courts shortlisted three candidates for any vacancies, but the central government made the final choice.

And there was absolutely no chance of conflicts of jurisdiction between these appeal courts and the local agents of central government, the prefects; whereas in the later years of the old regime there had been constant clashes between provincial parlements and the intendants. Tocqueville pointed out long ago that prefects were the lineal descendants of the intendants;[13] but they were both more and less. More, because their power in the departments they ruled was uncontested and uncontestable by anyone; less, because departments were almost always smaller than old regime generalities, and also because prefects enjoyed none of the initiative and local freedom of action that intendants had exercised, particularly in the last 40 years or so before the Revolution. Prefects were not expected to take initiatives. Their job was to provide constant and accurate information on their departments, and to implement and enforce the imperial will at that level. They were conceived as cogs in a uniform machine – and certainly not originators of any action that higher authority might not want to take responsibility for.

It was, then, from top to bottom, a political culture of obedience. There was no space anywhere for opposition to or even public discussion of whatever the government decided to do. Napoleon shared the widespread conviction that the old order had fallen because government had lost control of public opinion to irresponsible writers peddling utopian dreams, the sort of 'ideologues' whom he so heartily and volubly despised. Accordingly, the Consulate was marked by wholesale forced closures and mergers of newspapers, a process which continued under the Empire. By 1810 there were only around ten political titles still being published in Paris, and Savary, the incoming minister of police, was determined to reduce them yet further. 'Their existence', he declared,[14] 'is a relic of the Revolution, it seems just to organise them according to the maxims and the forms of the monarchy.' By the end of the year only four tightly controlled periodicals were still appearing; and by then, too, there had been put in place a structure of inspection and censorship for all publications whose machinery was closely modelled on the old regime's directorship of bookselling, right down to the name (*direction de la librairie*). The difference was that censors had far less latitude than before. It was still possible for authors to slip through the net into print – or almost, as the famous case of Mme de Staël's *De l'Allemagne* showed. But the officials who allowed that to happen were mercilessly punished.[15]

Notoriously, Napoleon would employ men regardless of their previous political track record, so long as they agreed to serve him without question. When he became an emperor this requirement became distinctly more personal, and higher officials took their oaths with their hands clasped in his, like vassals swearing fealty. But service and obedience were not to be seen as their own reward. They needed to be publicly recognised by imperial largesse. At the highest level, these recompenses were substantial – *sénatoreries*, *majorats* and apanages in the outer reaches of the Empire, with important revenues. In a well-known letter to Joseph of 1806,[16] the Emperor spoke of raising up '100 fortunes, which have all been built up alongside the throne, and which are the only estates remaining of any size in the country', and entailed on the descendants of their owners. All of these would be required to reside in Paris, and dance attendance on the Emperor at court. Here were more signs of admiration for Louis XIV. It did not extend, it is true, to re-occupying Versailles. It was too redolent of the Bourbon monarchy. But older palaces like Fontainebleau were brought back into service, and in Paris there really was no realistic alternative to the Tuileries – from which anyway the last Bourbon monarch had been ignominiously bundled in a way the first Bonaparte did not intend to be repeated. But an emperor had to have a court, and a very lavish one at that; and it could not seem authentic without nobles. Some have seen the origins of the imperial nobility in the Legion of Honour, with its ranks and its red ribbon reminiscent of the old order of St. Louis abolished in 1791. These were certainly authentic echoes. But something like the Legion had been suggested quite early in the Revolution; and by a man, too, who had helped to abolish the old nobility.[17] The First Consul defended the Legion, when it was created, as eminently meritocratic and republican. It was only when the imperial nobility was created that the Legion of Honour began to be viewed as a sort of order of chivalry, whose higher ranks conferred imperial titles. The Imperial Nobility has often been identified as Napoleon's greatest betrayal of the Revolution. But once again, behind all the titles, heraldry and hierarchy so redolent of the world before an anti-aristocratic revolution, the imperial variant was a very different creature. There was no automatic heredity, except at the highest and most financially secure level. There was no entry by purchase, which had been the main way in before 1789. And although Napoleon tried to give it tone by recruiting into it as many appropriate *ci-devants* (like himself) as he could, there was no guaranteed entry for people whose nobility derived from other sources.[18]

One thing, however, the imperial nobility did share with its pre-revolutionary namesake: it had no collective representation or organisation. The nearest it came was in the Senate, which contained most of the Empire's greatest notables, all enjoying special titles and privileges. At the Restoration, the Imperial Senate made an effortless transition into the Chamber of Peers. But neither then nor under Napoleon was it deemed to *represent* anyone. It was an advisory and legislative body nominated by the ruler. So, under Napoleon, were the other legislative branches. The only representative in the Empire was the Emperor himself, whose position had been initially sanctioned and legitimised by the Nation in a plebiscite. And this could scarcely have been any other way, given how Napoleon had come to power in the first place, and the rationales he had used to justify his rule. The revolutionary attempt to establish viable parliamentary government had failed: that was the most basic premise of the whole Napoleonic epic. He had saved the country from the chaos that had ensued, and the Empire had been created to perpetuate that salvation. Any attempts by any of the chambers of nominees in the consular or the imperial legislative process to behave like elected representatives were sternly repressed; and in 1807 the Tribunate was abolished entirely while the Legislative Body was left to wither away.

Yet legislative assemblies proved a genuinely new reflex that the Revolution had established in France. Even Napoleon never felt able to dispense entirely with this novel element in French political culture. In one of his famous gnomic remarks, he said that his system would see him out, but that his successor would have to rule very differently. Presumably he meant more co-operatively. That successor was not the one he hoped and planned for. Napoleon II may have been called King of Rome – surely a deliberate affront to his mother's family whose heir presumptive to the crown of the old *Reich* had enjoyed the title of King of the Romans? – but he never came to sit on the throne of a French Empire. But even the Bourbon who did succeed as ruler of France realised that his restored monarchy would have to be parliamentary.

Paris today is still a city where echoes of Napoleon and images of him are everywhere and unavoidable, but there is one place where he is quite invisible. In the Palais Bourbon, seat of the National Assembly, there is no picture, no statue, no image of the First Republic's destroyer. The only visual allusion to him is a volume labelled 'Code' high up in a frescoed cornice; and even the Code was something he did not create, but only brought to final fruition. All this is entirely appropriate. For the National Assembly, an elected body of legislative representatives, is the legacy of the Revolution's distinctive contribution to accumulated French political culture, one that survived all the Emperor's attempts to wipe it out by creating an imperial monarchy more absolute than anything the Bourbons had ever dreamed of.

CHAPTER 13

Revolutionary Napoleon

Napoleon's meteoric career ended on 18 June 1815 with his defeat at the hands of the Duke of Wellington. The two of them never met, and the closest they ever came was on that fateful day, when they might have glimpsed each other through their field telescopes. And in all sorts of ways they could scarcely have been more different. True enough, they were almost exactly the same age. They were both of aristocratic extraction, but younger sons, both born on offshore islands ambivalent about their relationship with the mainland. But whereas Napoleon owed almost everything except his start in life to the opportunities offered him by a revolution which he played no part whatsoever in bringing about, or directing, until it was losing its momentum, Wellington rose as an insider, through the long-established mechanisms of the British old regime: an education at Eton, a military placement through the patronage network of an influential Anglo-Irish family, an experience of warfare built up over many years of fighting for King George III on the frontiers of his far-flung empire. Wellington always had an unshakeable belief in the systems – whether social, political, or military – through which he had risen to glory. He regarded himself as a gentleman, from a class born to rule. He was always convinced that Napoleon, or *Buonaparte* as he enjoyed calling him, was not.

And yet without Napoleon, Wellington's career as it developed would have been very different. No doubt his military achievements in India would still have been significant, but he would have remained the 'Sepoy General' that Napoleon always liked to call him, scarcely better remembered perhaps than Sir Eyre Coote, also one of the most consistently successful generals in British history, but whose triumphs were confined to the subcontinent. But Wellington, or at least the triumphant Wellington we remember, was made by the conflict with Napoleon. The Emperor's attempt to take over the Iberian peninsula gave Sir Arthur Wellesley the opportunity to demonstrate his military talents in a European context, not against maharajahs, but against first-rate French armies. And Napoleon's determination to make a comeback after his defeat and abdication in 1814 allowed the Duke of Wellington at last to cross swords with him in person, and crown his reputation as the man who finally put an end to the most amazing military career in history.

But what sort of an adversary did Wellington think he was fighting against? He recognised, of course, what a formidable military opponent Napoleon was. After one of his narrowest peninsular victories, he declared that if Boney had been there, he and his troops would have been 'beat'.[1] Napoleon's presence on any battlefield, he said, was worth 40,000 men;[2] although when he finally confronted him at Waterloo he seems to have been a little disappointed that all he faced from this artillery trained officer was hard pounding, albeit the heaviest and most nearly overwhelming pounding he had ever encountered. But these were technical and professional issues. Much more important was what Napoleon stood for, and here Wellington seems to have had little doubt. Napoleon was not, he said, a personality but a *principle*.[3] And the principle he stood for was the overthrow of every established authority in Europe except his own, and a complete contempt for all well-established ways of doing things. The rulers of Europe whose combined efforts finally brought him down, thought the same. Napoleon, a self-made usurper who always marched under the tricolour adopted as the flag of the regenerated French Nation in 1789, was a mortal threat to all prescriptive authority.

He himself said so. I am a son of the Revolution, he declared when he was First Consul. And looking back from St. Helena in 1815[4] he claimed that 'Nothing can destroy or efface the grand principles of our Revolution. These great and noble truths must remain forever, so inextricably are they linked to our splendour, our monuments, our prodigious deeds. We have drowned its earlier shame in floods of glory... these truths will rule the world. They will be the creed, the religion, the morality of all nations: and, no matter what has been said, this memorable era will be linked to my person, because, after all, I have carried its torch and consecrated its principles, and because persecution has now made me its Messiah. Friends and enemies, all will say I am its first soldier, its great representative.' It is equally true, of course, that in proclaiming the constitution which formally inaugurated the consulate in 1799, he had declared that the Revolution was over. But that was only, it was argued, because as a consequence of the new constitution, the Revolution was now established on the principles with which it began. And in any case, he was talking only about France. For all the sound and fury of the 1790s, the Revolution had had very little practical impact in Europe beyond, except west of the Rhine and in Italy. Only six years later would Napoleon begin to turn the rest of the continent upside down. But then, those who stood in his path would regard him as the Revolution incarnate.

And yet, Napoleon among many historians enjoys the reputation of a conservative, if not a reactionary. After all, was it not he who snuffed out the representative government and national sovereignty, those principles whose proclamation marked the revolutionary moment in 1789? Did he not extinguish the freedom of speech and publication which the Revolution had unlocked? Did he not destroy the political promise of the Republic by becoming a hereditary monarch, and making a dynastic marriage into the oldest ruling family in Europe? Did he not restore the established Catholic Church after the revolutionaries had proclaimed a secular, non-confessional state? And what about the meritocracy proclaimed by the Revolution, and its abolition of nobility? Did he not turn his back on that by re-establishing aristocracy? Those are the main charges, but others are sometimes added, such as his resolute restriction of the rights of women.

We can consider these powerful charges one by one, but first a more general point. If, as suggested earlier, there is an important sense in which Wellington was made by Napoleon, it is even more obvious that Napoleon was made by, and was a product of, the Revolution. Although as a nobleman and a graduate of exclusive military academies he was far from disadvantaged under the old regime, without the Revolution his fate would probably have been to moulder away his life as a relatively junior officer. He might legitimately have hoped to rise to the rank of major, but scarcely beyond, since as late as 1788 the organisational principle of the royal army was to keep higher commands in the hands of the so-called 'first' nobility of the court. Or if that had been too much for that prodigious energy to bear, the young Lieutenant Buonaparte might have gone home to Corsica (as he briefly did) and tried to organise a revolt against French rule. Even if that had succeeded, he would scarcely have been more than the footnote that his childhood hero Paoli would forever be in wider European history. But the Revolution, in shedding a huge range of senior officers through emigration, and then launching an open-ended war against the rest of Europe which demanded a rapid expansion of the armies, gave young officers who stayed with the colours the opportunity to rise to whatever level their talents would carry them. Napoleon had a natural aptitude for playing this game, and during his initial triumphs as a general in Italy, he began to acquire that taste for supremacy which he would pursue single-mindedly through until 18 June 1815. He owed it all, initially, to the unprecedented opportunities offered by the Revolution, and he never forgot or denied it. What is more, the French power that he wielded so confidently and ruthlessly after he took control, was infinitely greater than anything that the old monarchy had been able to command. The Revolution had unlocked resources in France that no other continental state could match, and gave whoever controlled them a huge competitive advantage. Ironically, the destruction which Napoleon later brought to the other old regimes of Europe helped to sweep away the same sort of impediments to the power of the state elsewhere; and so in the end, by strengthening them too, he hastened his own defeat. But in between, a career inconceivable without the Revolution was crowned by placing the energy and resources which it released fully at its beneficiary's disposal.

And so he never condemned the Revolution. First of all he saw condemnation as pointless. In 1808 he wrote:[5] 'We must avoid all reaction in speaking of the Revolution. No man could oppose it. Blame lies neither with those who perished nor those who have survived. There was no individual force capable of changing its elements or of preventing events which arose from the nature of things and from circumstances.' He was also prepared to acknowledge that without the Revolution he would never have got where he had. Nevertheless he thought that in certain crucial respects it had gone astray. The Terror, he thought, had brought shame on the country. Part of the justificatory myth which he built up so assiduously once in power was that he had saved France from relapsing into a new Terror amid the panic of defeat in 1798 and 1799. And he often compared himself favourably with

Oliver Cromwell, another soldier who had climbed to power in revolutionary circumstances, but who, he said, had killed far more people on the way up, and ruled far more repressively. But what he admired about Cromwell was the brisk way in which he dealt with parliamentary babblers. This was another thing Napoleon took pride in having saved France from. It was politicians, or, as he liked to call them, *idéologues*, who had got the country into such a mess in 1793–4, and failed to establish a stable new order in the aftermath of the Terror. He had the soldier's contempt for talking-shops, where nothing got done, and windbags wasted time and resources in useless discussion. So he never saw representative government as in any way the essence of the Revolution. In his view, as he wrote in a letter to Talleyrand as early as 1797,[6] 'The governmental power…ought to be regarded as the real representative of the nation.' It was the very attempt to make more widely representative institutions work which had got the Revolution into the series of deplorable messes which marked its history.

Nor could this be disentangled from the whole issue of freedom of speech and publication. Napoleon shared the widespread view of his time that the Revolution had been brought about by writers, particularly Rousseau, whom he had himself devoured in his youth, but later came to see as a mere talker, another ideologue. It would have been better for France, he said, if Jean-Jacques had never lived. Writers in general he saw as the scourge of a stable social and political life. They needed to be closely watched and controlled, or they would undermine all good order. And before condemning him, we should perhaps ask ourselves how committed the revolutionaries themselves had ever been to free expression of opinion. They retrospectively admired the writers of the Enlightenment, of course. Like Napoleon, they saw them as having played a crucial role on preparing the Revolution. But how could revolutionaries, whose legitimacy derived from an overthow, feel safe in allowing people opposed to that overthrow to express their opposition? So even their founding manifesto, the Declaration of the Rights of Man and the Citizen, only guaranteed freedom of expression insofar as it was exercised responsibly and did not trouble public order 'as established by law'. Many clearly thought that meant no right to criticise or oppose *any* law that the National Assembly had passed: it was after all the expression of the General Will, which Rousseau had taught them was never wrong. And so it was really only during the first two years of the Revolution, and in the two following the fall of Robespierre, that the French press was anything like free – and even then writers deemed extremists were constantly hassled by one form or another of intimidation. In this light, we might say that Napoleon's control of the media merely systematised some powerful revolutionary impulses. He himself said that in principle he was in favour of complete press freedom, but that a free press simply could not be trusted.[7] Meanwhile, what he claimed to have done was to rescue the essence of the Revolution from men, from ideas, and from unstable institutions, whose sole achievement had been to squander it.

And was that so absurd a claim? If the crucial revolutionary moment, the establishment of the essential principle that would underpin everything else, was the proclamation of national sovereignty, Napoleon's rule acknowledged that. The Consulate was marked by three fundamental constitutional changes: the constitution of 1799, the life consulship of 1802 (sometimes called the Constitution of the Year X), and the establishment of the Empire (ending the Consulate of course) in 1804. All three were endorsed by plebiscites – expressions, however flawed and rigged, of the sovereign Nation's will. Thereby Napoleon could claim that he ruled, even as a hereditary emperor, by popular consent. And while it is true that for the next ten years there were no more plebiscites, there were no further proposed changes in the constitution either. When truly constitutional change was next proposed, with the Additional Act of 1815 during the Hundred Days, that too was put to a hasty plebiscite. And although it is obviously true as well that the result of all these plebiscites, with their mountainous majorities, was about as convincing as the election of many another plebiscitary tyrant, it has been shown by Malcolm Crook, perhaps the first historian to take them seriously, that the process of casting plebiscitary votes offered considerable scope for voters to record their views, even dissident ones.[8] And why not let them? It was not as if they were going to be allowed to win in the end. Yet the fact that these consultations were held at all shows that Napoleon acknowledged what was then quite a new principle, first proclaimed in Europe by the French revolutionaries: that sovereign nations should decide on their own forms of government.

And if they decided on a form of monarchy, that was their right. Historians have too often assumed that the Revolution was republican from the start. But there was hardly any republicanism in 1789, and the original revolutionary project was to convert an absolute monarchy into a constitutional one. It was three years before it was recognised that the king on the throne was unprepared to sign up to that project; and the experience of trying to establish a republic between 1792 and 1794 was so bloody and traumatic that no sooner had the Terror ended than the Convention was holding out the possibility of a monarchical restoration. Once again it was only the refusal of the legitimate monarch, now Louis XVIII, to accept a constitutional role (by the Declaration of Verona in 1795) that pushed them into further fruitless attempts to make a republic work. One reason they failed, of course, was that huge numbers of the French persisted in wanting a monarch to rule them. When Napoleon offered himself in that role, most of them were satisfied. The evidence for that is the way that the royalist resistance and obstruction which had dogged the Revolution since 1793 very largely faded away.

It is true that this process was expedited by the resolution of the religious problem. The religious schism, originating with the Civil Constitution of the Clergy in 1790, was perhaps the most fundamental cleavage opened up by the Revolution. It allowed counter-revolutionaries to draft God on to their side, and drove the Convention eventually to proclaim that the French state had no religious affiliation – that prickly principle which still inflames political debate in France today. Many revolutionaries, particularly in the army, repeatedly brought in at home and abroad to deal with the fanatical followers of intransigent priests, saw the deal which Napoleon struck with the papacy in 1801 as a fundamental betrayal of what they had fought for. But what had triggered off the refusal, ultimately of around half the clergy of France, to swear allegiance to a constitution which subjected them to secular power was the refusal of Pope Pius VI to endorse the religious policy of the National Assembly. Napoleon's achievement (which he said was the most difficult thing he had ever accomplished) was to get a new pope to agree to almost everything his predecessor had rejected. In return for the restoration of public worship, acknowledgement of Rome's spiritual authority, and an undertaking to pay clerical wages, Pius VII recognised the loss of church lands, the redrawing of the ecclesiastical map, the loss of Avignon, the dissolution of the monasteries, equal treatment for other faiths, and the appointment of the clergy at every level by the secular power. It is true that they were not to be elected by the laity, as the Civil Constitution had ordained, but again the basic principle remained: that the church was to be to all intents and purposes an arm of the state and organised along the same broad lines. After 11 years of resistance, the Catholic Church surrendered to the French

Revolution and its ultimate spokesman: an atheist who believed that the mystery of religion was merely the mystery of the social order.

One of the objectives of the Civil Constitution of the Clergy was the rationalisation of the church's structure and organisation. Rationalisation was a principle which the men of 1789 hoped to bring to every corner of French life. Napoleon was entirely in sympathy with this. He believed that so far as was possible things should be simple, uniform, orderly, practical, and work in the same way wherever he ruled. Partly this was the natural inclination of a military man: but it was also the realisation that the reforms initiated by the Revolution were the only way for any modern state to go. The old regime had been chaotic, unsystematic, inequitable, inefficient and irrational. The revolutionaries had been determined to clean out this Augean stable, and where they had done so, for instance in the redrawing of the administrative map and the creation of *départements*, or the creation of a new tax structure, Napoleon simply accepted and built upon their work. Where they had merely begun, but for whatever reason failed to complete their reforms, he brought them into port. He confirmed the new decimal currency of francs and centimes, for instance. He gave full government backing to the metric system, that great and most enduring gift of the French Revolution to the world. One day it will be all conquering, and it was Napoleon who gave it its initial boost. And, perhaps most memorably, he brought to rapid completion the Civil Code, a great project of law codification that the French had been talking about since Louis XIV, and that the revolutionaries had undertaken to complete but never had. He took a personal role in this, presiding at a number of working sessions of the commission, but above all pushing the work relentlessly along to triumphant completion.

And in social and professional terms, there can be no doubt that Napoleon consolidated the aspirations and work of the

Revolution. All the revolutionary regimes except the Jacobin Convention between June 1793 and July 1794 were committed to the principle that only men of property should have any say in public life or right to public office. Even the Jacobins of the Year II adopted their ferocious populist rhetoric and vocal championing of the *sansculottes* more because they thought they had no real choice, sitting defenceless amid the bloodthirsty populace of Paris, than out of any basic conviction. Napoleon thought that governing in co-operation with the propertied classes, the 'granite masses' as he called them, was only common sense. The bedrock of all his social policies, which he even enshrined in the oath he took at his imperial coronation, was that the lands nationalised and resold under the Revolution, mostly at the expense of the church, could never be returned, but were safe in the hands of their new acquirers. But at the same time he was fiercely committed to the careers open to the talents which were enshrined in the Declaration of the Rights of Man and the Citizen in 1789 and its successors of 1793 and 1795. How could he not be, given his own career? He was anxious to promote and reward talent wherever he found it, both to consolidate loyalty to his own rule, and simply to promote its efficiency. Nor was he afraid, as many men of power are, to promote people of ability in case they threatened his own position. It never crossed his mind, at least after 1801, that anybody was remotely as able as he was.

The great objection to the idea of Napoleon as patron of meritocracy is, of course, his restoration of aristocracy in 1808. But in fact it was not a restoration.[9] Napoleon always claimed, indeed, that he created the imperial titular hierarchy in order to *supplant* the remnants of the old nobility by creating a more prestigious scale of honours. Napoleonic titles were not automatically hereditary. They conveyed no fiscal privileges, as old regime nobility had: in fact, they often went to the highest taxpayers. They could not be bought, as most old regime nobility was, through the sale of offices. For all his respect for wealth, Napoleon was always against any resurrection of the venality abolished in 1789. 'By my creation', he declared,[10] 'I managed to substitute positive and meritorious things for ancient and detested prejudices. My national titles re-established precisely that equality which feudal nobility had banished. All sorts of merit led there: for parchments I substituted fine actions and for private interests, the interests of the country. It was no longer in imaginary darkness, in the night of time, that pride would be shown, but rather in the finest pages of our history. In fact, I dispelled the shocking pretensions of bloodline; that absurd idea.' Officially, indeed, the new titular hierarchy was never called a nobility – until it was recognised as such, not by Napoleon himself, but by the restored Bourbons in the Charter of 1814. And when he was briefly restored in 1815, the Emperor, while creating a few new titles of his own, re-promulgated revolutionary legislation abolishing nobility and feudal rights.

Napoleon's hostility to rights for women, and to their involvement in public affairs, has always been notorious, and often seen as a spectacular backtracking on revolutionary commitments. But, as argued in a previous chapter,[11] the French Revolution actually offered women next to nothing. All they got out of it, and that a very ambiguous concession, was the right to divorce; and that came not from any concern about the plight of women, but rather as a mere spin-off from marriage being made a civil rather than a divine contract. Napoleon certainly went back on that. But if one of the main objectives of many revolutionaries was to deny women any access to the public sphere, and to reduce them to a position of subservience unprecedented even under the old regime, Napoleon's attitudes were entirely in line with those aspirations.

Sooner or later, revolutions have to end. French revolutionaries of one sort or another had been claiming, usually more in hope than conviction, that the Revolution was over, or soon would be, since at least 1791. But it was only Napoleon who managed to bring about that closure, by sewing up the gaping wounds that it had opened in French life. His stitches were sometimes rough and painful, but by and large they held. Meanwhile, we should make a distinction between ending the Revolution and betraying it. The aim of all the revolutionaries was to end it, by establishing a new order, along new lines. Those lines were amply sketched out, and the foundations laid. The problem that eluded them was to give the new edifice stability. Napoleon's great contribution was to provide that. So he really did establish the Revolution, at least on *most* of the principles with which it began. And after half a generation's consolidation under his firm hand, they could not be uprooted, even by the restored Bourbons. As has often been said, Louis XVIII did not ascend the throne of his dead brother, but that of Napoleon.

So much for France. But everybody in the 1790s, and not just the revolutionaries of France, was convinced that the effects of what the French were trying to do could not be confined to their own country. The principles which they espoused were universal ones, applicable everywhere, nothing less than the Rights of Man. Within months of going to war in 1792, they were proclaiming that their war aims were to overthrow old regimes everywhere and to help oppressed foreigners to establish the rule of liberty and equality. The young general Bonaparte played an important role in this campaign, a revolutionary warlord who turned northern Italy upside down in 1796 and 1797. But much of what he had achieved was reversed over the next couple of years while he was away in Egypt, and only in the Netherlands did French ways and principles durably replace former authorities and institutions. Not until 1801 was the situation as the hero of Italy had left it four years earlier restored, as the second coalition fell apart, and the wars of the French Revolution came to an end. When they did, the France of the First Consul dominated Europe militarily. Even the British had given up most of the gains of a decade in the Peace of Amiens. Nevertheless most of the old states of Europe were still standing, battered but unbowed. Only the thrones of the Dutch Stadtholder and a handful of German prince-bishops had disappeared through opposing the French. The most spectacular royal casualty of the 1790s, the king of Poland, had been the victim not of French power but of other monarchs, rulers deriving their legitimacy from the old regime.

The new series of conflicts that began in 1803, and exploded in 1805, is properly called the Napoleonic wars. They were different from the wars of the French Revolution in that they were either instigated by Napoleon or waged to curb his ambitions. And as far as the other rulers of Europe were concerned, they were fought against an upstart, a usurper, a ruler whose only legitimacy lay in the armed force at his command. Yet that force was ultimately derived from the Revolution. Napoleon knew that other monarchs despised him, and only dealt with him on sovereign terms because they had no choice. But since force was the only weapon he had, he used it ruthlessly. And so it was he, not the Revolution directly, who destroyed the old regime in most of the rest of Europe. It was this monarch, who derived his legitimacy from the votes of a sovereign nation, who deposed the Bourbons of Naples and of Spain, and the House of Savoy in Alpine Italy, dispossessed the Habsburgs, Hohenzollerns and even the Hanoverians of vast swathes of ancestral territories, annexed the papal states, and forced the dissolution of the oldest political entity in Europe, the Holy Roman Empire of the German Nation. In those areas which he annexed to the French Empire, in Italy, Germany and the Netherlands, the full range of rationalisations pioneered in France was introduced. That meant new *départements*, uniform taxes and tariffs, and conscription – another revolutionary innovation that Napoleon took over and made permanent. It meant the Code and new courts to enforce it, and (in Catholic regions) the Concordat. And all this was accomplished, as the work of Michael Broers has emphasised,[12] through a corps of administrators and collaborators who believed in what he and they were doing, men who had seen the French Revolution as a great clearing of the jungle of the old regime to make way for the seeding of more rational and enlightened values. They were hated for the changes which they exulted in imposing, just as educated, rationalising revolutionaries had been hated throughout much of France in the 1790s. Long mesmerised by the populism which a few thousand *sansculottes* of Paris forced the Convention into in 1793–94, historians have only come to recognise relatively recently how widespread resistance to the Revolution was among ordinary people in France itself, and some have argued that the true popular movement in France in the 1790s was counter- or at least anti-revolutionary.[13] But as then, popular resistance to the forces of change now represented by Napoleon proved unavailing, except perhaps in Spain, where his opponents had the alliance of British armies. Old ways, old beliefs, old organisations could not withstand the shock of French power. It was the Revolution that accomplished that in France. It was Napoleon who did it outside.

What enabled him to do so was that he always fought to achieve total victory. That too was revolutionary. Under the old regime, states fought for advantage, but statesmen recognised that the basis for durable peace when the fighting ended was to give all parties, even losers, some interest in the durability of whatever settlement was reached. But the message of the French Revolution was absolute: there could be no compromise with the forces of the old regime. That intransigence was one reason why it led to terror. Napoleon made war in the same way. He did not manoeuvre for advantage. He always went for total victory by *Blitzkrieg*, resulting in complete annihilation of the enemy's forces. He would then dictate terms, and he never dreamed of giving any defeated enemy a vested interest in the result, except fear of further humiliation. The Duke of Wellington, to return to him, understood this. 'If you look through his campaigns', he said,[14] 'you will find that his plan always was to try to give a great battle, gain a great victory, patch up a peace, such a peace as might leave an opening for a future war, and then hurry back to Paris.' But this was not a formula for durable stability, especially when he took on enemies against whom *Blitzkrieg* was ineffective: the British in their island, the Russians in their endless territory, the people of Spain, and Wellington himself, that master of defence and strategic retreat. And Napoleon's inability to master them gave continual hope, and eventually the opportunity of recovery, to those cowed adversaries whom he *had* been able to smash. All these forces combined in the end to defeat him, but even when he was defeated, former patterns and habits were so thoroughly shattered that they could never be put together again.

And not just in Europe. Although Napoleon's worldwide ambitions, never more than episodic, were consistently thwarted by the power of the British navy, this did not mean that his activities were without revolutionary consequences. His expedition to Egypt while he was still a revolutionary general destabilised a whole swathe of the Ottoman Empire and left Egypt ungovernable in the old terms. He had destroyed the old Mameluke military caste which had previously ruled there, and the general sent by the Ottomans to re-establish their control, Mehmet Ali, used his power to establish a dynasty of his own and a state partly modelled on French examples. Across the Atlantic, Napoleon's abortive attempt to revive the old slave-based French Caribbean empire by the reconquest of Saint-Domingue led directly to the declaration of independence by Haiti, a free black state of former slaves. His reinstitution of slavery in 1802, incidentally, is often held up as yet another betrayal of the revolutionary legacy. Yet moves against slavery were never taken seriously by successive revolutionary assemblies, and when in February 1794 the Convention abolished slavery in French territories, it was less the result of conviction than of a *fait accompli* by their representatives on the ground in Saint-Domingue, who had found that to abolish slavery was the only policy with a hope of keeping the colony French.[15] Here again, then, the First Consul was fully in tune with the revolutionary mainstream. But perhaps Napoleon's biggest impact across the Atlantic was to destabilise the two great Iberian empires when he invaded Spain and Portugal.[16] In the Portuguese case the trauma was postponed because the British managed to ship the king and his family out to Brazil before the invaders arrived. Even so the first residence of a European monarchy in its colonies brought all sorts of structural problems which in half a generation produced the separation of Brazil from Portuguese rule. In the Spanish empire the effect was more radical and immediate. The removal by Napoleon of the legitimate and never-contested monarchy in Madrid left a vacuum of power and authority wherever its writ had run, a classic trigger for revolutions. The result was, that in a wide variety of situations throughout Spanish America, power fell into local hands in ways that could not be reversed when the legitimate king recovered his throne back in Spain. In other words, the revolutions which brought about the independence of Latin America were unimaginable without the role played, thousands of miles away, by Napoleon.

If we tie the description revolutionary too closely to what happened in France in the Year II, then obviously Napoleon's claims are tenuous. He condemned and deplored the bloodshed and popular anarchy (as he saw it) of 1793–94, and repudiated most of the populist measures taken in that context, many of them often approvingly depicted since by historians as 'anticipations' of later egalitarian and socialist triumphs.[18] But this definition, which lies at the heart of the classic interpretation of the Revolution which has in any case crumbled away over the last half century, seems far too narrow and specific. Without Napoleon, many of the original aspirations of those who made the Revolution might never have established themselves permanently in France. Without Napoleon, the *anciens régimes* of Europe beyond might have lumbered along for generations more. Without Napoleon, the same might have happened in the Middle East and Latin America. This is not to say, far from it, that his downfall was a tragic loss for the world. And it is hard to believe that the Empire of Napoleon had any ultimate chance of permanence. The man himself was never satisfied with anything. But by the time he disappeared, he had certainly transformed everything that he touched. And after him, nothing that had existed before his touch could ever be the same again. If that cannot be called revolutionary, it is hard to say what could.

Notes

Chapter 1. Colbert and the Sale of Offices

This chapter is a translation of 'Colbert et les Offices' first published in *Histoire Économie et Société*, 19 (2000), pp.469–480. I am grateful to the journal's publisher, SEDES, for permission to reproduce it, and to Jean-Pierre Poussou for the invitation to write it.

1. K.W. Swart, *Sale of Offices in the Seventeenth Century* (The Hague, 1949); I. Mieck (ed.) *Ämterhändel im Spätmittelalter und im 16. Jahrhundert* (Berlin, 1984).
2. Richard Bonney, *The King's Debts. Finance and Politics in France, 1589–1661* (Oxford, 1981), pp.176–177.
3. William Doyle, *La Vénalité* (Paris, 2000), p.58.
4. Pierre Clément, *Histoire de la vie et de l'administration de Colbert* (Paris, 1846), pp.80–81.
5. Bonney, *The King's Debts*, pp.186–189; Daniel Dessert, *Argent, pouvoir et société au grand siècle* (Paris, 1984), pp.325–338.
6. Albert N. Hamscher, *The Parlement of Paris after the Fronde, 1653–1673* (Pittsburgh, 1976), pp.10–11.
7. Bonney, *The King's Debts*, pp.254–257.
8. Pierre Clément (ed.) *Lettres, Instructions et Mémoires de Colbert* (Paris, 1861), 7 vols, vii, pp.179–180.
9. Ibid., p.17.
10. Jean Lognon (ed.) *Mémoires de Louis XIV* (Paris, 1927), p.14.
11. Ibid., p.17.
12. Ibid., p.39.
13. Clément, *Lettres*, ii, pp.60–61.
14. Ibid.
15. Jean Nagle in M. Pinet (ed.) *Histoire de la fonction publique en France* (Paris, 1993), 2 vols, ii, p.190.
16. Hamscher, *Parlement of Paris*, p.65.
17. Dessert, *Argent, pouvoir et société*, ch.xi.
18. Clément, *Lettres*, vi, p.3. Colbert to the king, 22 October 1664.
19. F. Véron de Forbonnais, *Recherches et considérations sur les finances de France depuis l'année 1595 jusqu'à 1721* (Bâle, 1758), 2 vols, i, pp.328–329; Nagle in *Histoire de la fonction publique*, i, p.185.
20. Forbonnais, *Recherches*, i, p.328.

21.   Clément, *Histoire de Colbert* (2nd edn. 1874), ii, pp.421–422.

22.   Clément, *Lettres*, vi, p.247.

23.   Dessert, p.338.

24.   Hamscher, p.15.

25.   Ibid., p.21; John J. Hurt, *Louis XIV and the Parlements. The Assertion of Royal Authority* (Manchester, 2002), pp.21–22, 76–78.

26.   *Mémoires de Louis XIV*, pp.153–154.

27.   Hamscher, p.23.

28.   Ibid., p.24; Hurt, *Louis XIV and the Parlements*, pp.77–78.

29.   John Hurt, 'The Parlement of Brittany and the Crown, 1665–1675' in Raymond F. Kierstead (ed.) *State and Society in Seventeenth Century France* (New York, 1975), pp.53–55.

30.   Nagle in *Histoire de la fonction publique*, ii, p.187.

31.   Clément, *Histoire de Colbert* (1874 edn.), ii, p.421.

32.   Paul Sonnino, *Louis XIV and the Origins of the Dutch War* (Cambridge, 1988), ch.3.

33.   Clément, *Lettres,* ii, cix. Colbert to the Governor of Lyon, 20 December 1670.

34.   Forbonnais, i, pp.466–467.

35.   Ibid., p.468.

36.   Margaret and Richard Bonney, *Jean-Roland Malet, premier historien des finances de la monarchie française* (Paris, 1993), p.205.

37.   Sonnino, *Louis XIV and the Origins*, p.172.

38.   Forbonnais, i, p.275.

39.   Forbonnais, p.475, lists many of them.

40.   Clément, *Lettres*, ii, p.301. Letter to Intendants, 22 November 1673.

41.   Hamscher, pp.25–26.

42.   Clément, *Lettres*, ii, p.367. Circular to Intendants, 18 December 1674 p.369; Colbert to Prime President of the Parlement of Rennes, 28 December 1674; Hurt, *Louis XIV and the Parlements*, pp.68–69.

43.   Forbonnais, i, p.483.

44.   William Doyle, *Venality. The Sale of Offices in Eighteenth Century France* (Oxford, 1996), p.24.

45.   It is true that Colbert was probably unaware of the cardinal's ambivalent attitude towards venality, which remained unknown to the public until the publication of his *Testament politique* in 1688, five years after Colbert's death.

46.   Clément, *Lettres*, ii, p.127. 'Mémoire pour rendre compte au Roy de l'Estat de ses Finances'.

47.   With the possible exception of John Law, who made a passing reference, at the height of his 'System' in March 1720, to a total abolition. But by then this was probably a desperate expedient for keeping up the credit of the System at a moment when confidence was beginning to waver. See Edgar Faure, *17 juillet 1720: la banqueroute de Law* (Paris, 1976), p.403.

48.   The much-trumpeted abolitions of Maupeou in the 1770s, for example, only got rid of about 3,500 offices, or perhaps 2.5 per cent of the total in existence at the time: Doyle, *Venality*, p.118.

49.   Quoted by Jean Nagle in *Histoire de la fonction publique*, ii, p.159.

50. See Paul Sonnino, 'Jean-Baptiste Colbert and the origins of the Dutch War' *European Studies Review*, xiii (1983), pp.1–11.

51. *Argent, pouvoir et société*, p.137.

Chapter 2. Voltaire and Venality: The Ambiguities of an Abuse

This chapter first appeared in T.D. Hemming, E. Freeman and D. Meakin (eds.) *The Secular City. Studies in the Enlightenment presented to Haydn Mason* (Exeter, 1994). I am grateful to Haydn Mason for bibliographical suggestions.

1. *Les Caractères*, 'Du mérite personnel'.
2. René Pomeau, *D'Arouet à Voltaire 1694–1734* (Oxford, 1985), pp.16, 28, 30.
3. Ibid., p.16.
4. See François Bluche, *Les Magistrats du Parlement de Paris au xviiᵉ siècle 1715–1770* (Besançon, 1960), pp.245–246; Theodore Besterman, *Voltaire* (London, 1969), pp.38–39.
5. The standard account of these early stages is Roland Mousnier, *La Vénalité des offices sous Henri IV et Louis XIII* (Paris, 2ⁿᵈ edn., 1971).
6. Forbonnais, *Recherches et considérations*, i, p.329.
7. See ch.1, above.
8. Charles Loyseau, *Cinq livres du droit des offices* (Châteaudun, 1610), p.290.
9. Calculated from B[ibliothèque] N[ationale] MS Fr. 11103, 'Mémoire des Affaires Extraordinaires des Finances faites depuis 1687 jusqu'en 1705' and MS Fr. 11107, 'Recueil des Affaires Extraordinaires des Finances depuis et compris l'année 1706 jusqu'au [sic] présente année 1715'.
10. Forbonnais, *Recherches*, ii, p.395.
11. *État Général des Dettes de l'État à la mort du feu Roy Louis XIV* (Paris, 1720), p.25.
12. BN MS Fr. 11140, 'Mémoire sur l'état actuel des offices, tant casuels qu'à survivance'. Another version, different in detail and dated 1779, in MS Fr. 14084.
13. See William Doyle, '4 August 1789: the intellectual background to the abolition of venality of offices', *Australian Journal of French Studies* (1992), pp.230–240.
14. Necker estimated them in 1785 at precisely the same amount, 585 millions: see *A Treatise on the Finances of France, in three volumes by Mr. Necker* (London, 1785), I, p.37.
15. M. Pardessus (ed.) *Œuvres complètes du Chancelier d'Aguesseau* (Paris, 1819), 16 vols, xiii, p.224. See too Pierre Combe, *Mémoire inédit du Chancelier Daguesseau sur la réformation de la justice* (Valence, 1928), p.11.
16. Theodore Besterman (ed.) *Voltaire's Correspondence and Related Documents* (Geneva/Banbury, 1968–77), 50 vols, [abbreviated hereafter as Best.] letter 2035, 21 June 1739.

17. Besterman, *Voltaire*, pp.278–279; *Autobiography*, ibid., p.562.
18. *Le Siècle de Louis XIV*, ch.xxx.
19. *Essai sur les mœurs,* ch.cxiv; *Histoire du Parlement de Paris,* ch.xvi.
20. See the preface to the standard edition of the *Testament* by Louis André (Paris, 1947), pp.50–51.
21. *Considérations sur le gouvernement ancien et présent de la France* (Amsterdam, 1764), p.155 ff. Manuscript copies had circulated for almost 30 years before this posthumous publication.
22. Letter cited above, n.16. See also the *Autobiography* in Besterman, *Voltaire,* p.565.
23. *Des Mensonges imprimés, et du Testament politique du Cardinal de Richelieu.*
24. *Lettre sur le Testament politique du Cardinal Richelieu* (Paris, 1750). See also André, pp.51–52.
25. As d'Argenson, whose *Considérations* were printed at last in that same year.
26. Ch.xix.
27. (1771). Article 'Lois, Esprit des Lois'.
28. See Furio Diaz, *Filosofia e Politica nel settecento francese* (Turin, 1962), ch.vi.
29. See Peter Gay, *Voltaire's Politics. The Poet as Realist* (Princeton, 1959), ch.vii.
30. Ibid., p.317; see too Beuchot's introduction to his edition of the *Histoire*, 1829.
31. See [Louis Petit de Bachaumont], *Mémoires secrets pour servir à l'histoire de la république des lettres en France, depuis MDCCLXII jusqu'à nos jours* (London, 1780–1789), 36 vols, iv, 25 June 1769.
32. Ch.iv.
33. See below, p.36.
34. Presumably this means Montesquieu.
35. See William Doyle, 'The Parlements of France and the breakdown of the Old Regime' *French Historical Studies*, vi (1970), pp.414–458, reprinted in *Officers, Nobles and Revolutionaries. Essays on eighteenth century France* (London, 1995), pp.1–47. The fullest treatment of Voltaire's attitude to the Maupeou reforms is now James Hanrahan, *Voltaire and the parlements of France* (*SVEC* , Oxford, 2009, no.6), ch.6.
36. Best. 12114 and 12115.
37. Best. 12333.
38. Best. 12231 to Marin, 27 January 1771. See also Durand Echeverria, *The Maupeou Revolution. A Study in the History of Libertarianism. France, 1770–1774* (Baton Rouge, LA, 1985), p.148.
39. *Très humbles et très respectueuses remontrances d'un Grenier à Sel.* See also David Hudson, 'In defense of reform: French government propaganda during the Maupeou crisis' *French Historical Studies*, viii (1973), pp.67–68.
40. *Réponse aux remontrances de la Cour des Aides par un membre des nouvelles cours souveraines.*
41. Much of this passage was later incorporated into later editions of the *Dictionnaire philosophique.*
42. See Diaz, *Filosofia*, pp.458–465; Echeverria, *Maupeou Revolution*, chs.8 and 9; and John Lough, *The Philosophes and post-revolutionary France* (Oxford, 1982), pp.20–23.

43. 'Observations sur le Nakaz', no. xviii in Pierre Vernière (ed.) *Diderot: Œuvres politiques* (Paris, 1963), p.363.
44. Echeverria, *Maupeou Revolution*, pp.151–152.
45. Best. 13863, to d'Hornoy, 5 September 1774.
46. See Doyle, *Venality,* pp.279–311.
47. Mousnier, *La Vénalité*, pp.13–24.
48. Doyle, '4 August 1789', pp.234–236. But Voltaire's influence can be seen in other ways. Among the *Éloges de Montesquieu* submitted in an essay competition set by the Academy of Bordeaux in the 1780s, several cited Voltaire's criticism to show that even Montesquieu's judgement could sometimes be flawed. Bibliothèque de la Ville de Bordeaux, MS 828 (xcvi and xcvii). One of the authors was Bertrand Barère, the future revolutionary.

Chapter 3. Secular Simony: The Clergy and the Sale of Offices in Eighteenth-Century France

This chapter first appeared in Nigel Aston (ed.) *Religious Change in Europe 1650–1914. Essays for John McManners* (Oxford, 1997), pp.135–148. It is here reprinted with some slight amendments. I am grateful to Nigel Aston for the invitation to contribute to that volume.

1. Acts 8:9–24.
2. See R.A. Ryder, *Simony: An Historical Synopsis and Commentary* (Washington, DC, 1931).
3. Aristotle, *Politics*, bk. ii, ch.11; Plato, *Republic*, bk. vii, section 4.
4. Doyle, *Venality*, ch.10.
5. See R. Doucet, *Les institutions de la France au XVIᵉ siècle* (Paris, 1948), 2 vols, p.406.
6. Marcel Marion, *Les institutions de la France aux XVIIᵉ et XVIIIᵉ siècles* (Paris, 1923), p.406. See also, on conditional resignations in the church, C. Berthelot du Chesnay, 'Le Clergé diocésain français' *Revue d'histoire moderne et contemporaine*, x (1963), pp. 241–249.
7. The precise date has never been established: see Mousnier, *La Vénalité*, pp.44–45.
8. Ibid., pp. 38, 42, 62, 332, 338, 609.
9. Ibid., pp. 645–646.
10. *Maximes d'État, ou Testament politique d'Armand du Plessis, Cardinal Duc de Richelieu* (Paris, 1764), 2 vols, i, p. 201.
11. See Doyle, *Venality*, ch.7.
12. Mousnier, *La Vénalité*, p.31.
13. William Doyle, *The Parlement of Bordeaux and the End of the Old Regime, 1771–1790* (London, 1974), p. 43; François Bluche, *Les Magistrats du Parlement de Paris au XVIIIᵉ siècle (1715–1771)* (Paris, 1960), p.49. Bluche

attributes all to the *grand'chambre*, but elsewhere he makes it clear that (as in other parlements) no chamber had a fixed complement of clerics. But clerics served long, so most were likely to be in the *grand'chambre*.

14. Bluche, *Magistrats*, pp.55, 64–65.
15. Doyle, *Parlement of Bordeaux*, p.43.
16. Maurice Gresset, *Gens de Justice à Besançon, 1674–1789* (Paris, 1978), 2 vols, p.41.
17. Doyle, *Parlement of Bordeaux*, pp.28–29; Bluche, *Magistrats*, p.165.
18. Ibid., p.58.
19. Ibid., pp.170–172; Bailey Stone, *The French Parlements and the Crisis of the Old Regime* (Chapel Hill, NC, 1986), pp.55–56.
20. Ibid., pp.219–221.
21. Ibid., p.63.
22. Bluche, *Magistrats*, p.63.
23. Michel Antoine, *Le Conseil du Roi sous le règne de Louis XV* (Paris, 1970), pp.187–188. See also from the same author *Le Gouvernement et l'administration sous Louis XV: dictionnaire biographique* (Paris, 1978), pp.33–34, 227. Unusually Abbé Bertin was an elder brother.
24. Bachaumont, *Mémoires secrets*, xvii, 25 July 1781. See also Bailey Stone, *The Parlement of Paris, 1774–1789* (Chapel Hill, NC, 1981), p.25.
25. M. de Lescure (ed.) *Correspondance secrète inédite sur Louis XVI, Marie-Antoinette, la cour et la ville* (Paris, 1866), 2 vols, ii, p.6. 18 January 1786.
26. On the problem of identifying them, see Dale Van Kley, *The Jansenists and the Expulsion of the Jesuits from France 1757–1765* (New Haven, CT, 1975), ch.2.
27. On Chauvelin, see ibid., pp.50–51; on Nigon de Berty, see Bernard de Lacombe, *la Résistance Janséniste et parlementaire au temps de Louis XV: l'Abbé Nigon de Berty (1702–1774)* (Paris, 1948).
28. See Van Kley, *The Jansenists*, pp.109–112, and Julian Swann, *Politics and the Parlement of Paris under Louis XV, 1754–1774* (Cambridge, 1995), pp.206–213.
29. See Van Kley, *The Jansenists*, pp.50–51.
30. *Institutions d'un prince, ou traité des qualitez des vertus et des devoirs d'un souverain, soit par rapport au gouvernement temporel de ses états, ou comme chef d'une société chrétienne qui est nécessairement liée avec la religion. En quatre parties* (London, 1739). See Alexander Sedgwick, *Jansenism in seventeenth century France: Voices from the Wilderness* (Charlottesville, VA, 1977), pp.182–187.
31. *Institutions d'un prince*, ch.6.
32. Ibid., p.164.
33. Ibid., pp.163, 167.
34. *Mémoire pour diminuer le nombre des procès* (Paris, 1725), pp.225–226.
35. Ibid., p.226; *Maximes d'État*, p.200.
36. *Politics*, ii, ch.11.
37. *Mémoire*, pp.229–230.
38. See A. Chérel, *Fénelon au XVIIIᵉ siècle en France (1715–1820)* (Paris, 1917), pp.339–343.

39. 'Lettre à Louis XIV' in C. Urbain (ed.) *Fénelon: écrits et lettres politiques* (Paris, 1920), pp.48–49.

40. 'Plans de gouvernement concertés avec le duc de Chevreuse pour être proposés au duc de Bourgogne' in ibid., pp.117,120, 122.

41. See Doyle '4 August 1789' in *Officers, Nobles and Revolutionaries*, pp.141–153; and above, p.38.

42. 'Réflexions sur la vénalité des charges en France' in *Histoire de l'Académie Royale des Inscriptions et Belles Lettres avec les Mémoires de Littérature tirés des registres de cette Académie depuis l'année MCCCXLIX jusque et compris l'année MDCCI*, xxiii, pp.278–283.

43. BN MSS Fr. n.a. 2495, fo.129. Bertin was not related to the comptroller-general and his clerical brother of the same surname mentioned above.

44. See above, p.37.

45. See Beatrice Fry Hyslop, *A Guide to the General Cahiers of 1789* (New York, 1968), p.144. Most of the texts are to be found in the first six volumes of J. Madival and F. Laurent (eds.) *Archives parlementaires de 1787 à 1869* (Paris, 1879), 90 vols (hereafter, *AP*).

46. Ibid., iii, pp.590–591.

47. Ibid., p.659.

48. See Doyle, *Officers, Nobles and Revolutionaries*, pp.149–151.

49. *AP*, i, p.291.

50. *AP*, v, p.649, Clergy of Saint-Quentin.

51. See above, p.37.

52. e.g. *AP*, iii, p.403, Nobility of Gien.

53. On this process and its vicissitudes, see Doyle, *Venality*, ch.9.

Chapter 4. Changing Notions of Public Corruption
(*c.*1770–*c.*1850)

This chapter first appeared in Emmanuel Kreike and William Chester Jordan (eds.) *Corrupt Histories* (Rochester, NY, 2004). I am grateful to the editors for permission to reprint it, and to Professor Jordan for the invitation to present the original version at the Shelby Cullom Davis Center for Historical Studies, Princeton University, in 1999.

1. Anthony Bruce, *The Purchase System in the British Army 1660–1871* (London, 1980).

2. 'Observations sur le Nakaz' xviii, in P. Vernière (ed.) *Diderot: Œuvres politiques* (Paris, 1963), pp.364–365.

3. W. D. Rubinstein, 'The end of "old corruption" in Britain, 1780–1860' *Past and Present*, 101 (1963), pp.55–86; Philip Harling, *The Waning of 'Old Corruption': the Politics of Economical Reform in Britain 1779–1846* (Oxford, 1996).

4. Rubinstein, 'End of "Old Corruption"', p.78.
5. Plato, *Republic*, bk.8; Aristotle, *Politics*, bk.2, ch.11.
6. Doyle, *Venality*, ch.8.
7. See Joel Hurstfield, 'Political Corruption in Modern England: the Historian's Problem', in *Freedom, Corruption and Government in Elizabethan England* (London, 1973), pp.137–162.
8. *De l'Esprit des lois*, bk.5, ch.19.
9. See Doyle, *Venality*, pp.240–242.
10. *Decline and Fall of the Roman Empire*, ch.21.
11. *Essays*, 6, 'Of the Independency of Parliament'. The italics are Hume's.
12. John Brewer, *The Sinews of Power: War, Money and the English State 1688–1783* (London, 1988).
13. Doyle, *Venality*, pp.104–105, 134–136.
14. Bruce, *Purchase System*, passim.
15. G.C. Bolton, *The Passing of the Irish Act of Union: a Study of Parliamentary Politics* (Oxford, 1966).
16. Sir Norman Chester, *The English Administrative System 1780–1870* (Oxford, 1981), ch.4.
17. Ibid., p.166.
18. Harling, *Waning of 'Old Corruption'*, p.189.
19. Ibid., pp.104–106, 261–262.
20. Ian Bradley, *The Call to Seriousness: The Evangelical Impact on the Victorians* (London, 1976); Boyd Hilton, *The Age of Atonement: The Influence of Evangelicalism on Social and Economic Thought, 1795–1865* (Oxford, 1988).
21. See William Doyle, *Origins of the French Revolution*, 3rd edn. (Oxford, 1999), pp.5–41.
22. Doyle, *Venality*, ch.8.
23. Ibid., pp.268–73.
24. Ibid., ch.8.
25. See above, 'Voltaire and Venality,' *passim*.
26. Doyle, *Venality*, ch.9.
27. Chester, *English Administrative System*, pp.125–130.
28. Bolton, *Passing of the Irish Act of Union*, p.161.
29. Ibid., pp.205–207.
30. A.S. Turberville, *The House of Lords in the Age of Reform 1784–1837* (London, 1958), p.478.
31. *From Max Weber: Essays in Sociology* (eds. H.H. Gerth and C. Wright Mills) (London, 1948), pp.196–244.
32. Chester, *English Administrative System*, pp.142–555, traces the evolution of a salaried administration, 1780–1870.
33. Clive H. Church, *Revolution and Red Tape. The French Ministerial Bureaucracy, 1770–1850* (Oxford, 1981), ch.8.
34. Chester, *English Administrative System*, pp.155–166.
35. Church, *Revolution and Red Tape*, pp.296–306.
36. *Waning of 'Old Corruption'*, pp.265–266.

Chapter 5. The Union with Ireland in a European Context

This chapter first appeared in *Transactions of the Royal Historical Society,* 6th Series, 10 (2000). I am grateful to Cambridge University Press for permission to reprint this slightly amended version. It was first presented at a conference in Belfast in 1999 to mark the bicentenary of the Act of Union. I am grateful to the late Professor Peter Jupp for the invitation to present it.

1. The most convenient general survey of these complexities is Maurice Bordes, *L'Administration provincial et municipal en France au XVIIIe siècle* (Paris, 1972).
2. H.G. Koenigsberger, 'Dominium regale or dominium politicum et regale' (1975) in *Politicians and Virtuosi. Essays in Early Modern History* (London, 1986), pp.1–25; J.H. Elliott, 'A Europe of Composite Monarchies' *Past and Present,* 137 (1992), pp.48–71; D.W. Hayton, James Kelly and John Bergin (eds.) *The Eighteenth Century Composite State. Representative Institutions in Ireland and Europe, 1689–1800* (Basingstoke, 2010).
3. Henry Kamen, *The War of Succession in Spain, 1700–1715* (London, 1969), pp.299–307.
4. J.G. Simms, *William Molyneux of Dublin, 1656–1698* (Dublin, 1982).
5. William Molyneux, *The Case of Ireland's being bound by acts of parliament in England, stated* (Dublin, 1698).
6. J.C.D. Clark, *English Society 1660–1832* (Cambridge, 1985, 2nd edn. 2000).
7. Although not enshrined in the Act of Union, the terms North and South Britain were regularly employed in eighteenth-century Acts of Parliament.
8. Simms, *Molyneux,* pp.104–105.
9. W.E.H. Lecky, *A History of Ireland in the Eighteenth Century* (London, 1902), 5 Vols, i, pp.443–444.
10. R.F. Foster, *Modern Ireland, 1600–1922* (London, 1988), ch.8.
11. Simms, *Molyneux,* pp.104–106.
12. Richard Butterwick, *Poland's Last King and English Culture* (Oxford, 1988), pp.26–27; Henry Marczali, *Hungary in the Eighteenth Century* (Cambridge, 1910), pp.102–106.
13. King Stanislas Poniatowski himself described Stackelberg, the Russian ambassador, as 'the proconsul': S. Goryainov et al. (eds.) *Mémoires du roi Stanislas-Auguste Poniatowski* (St. Petersburg/Leningrad, 1914–1924), 2 vols, ii, 298. I am grateful to Richard Butterwick for this reference.
14. R.R. Palmer, *The Age of the Democratic Revolution 1769–1800* (Princeton, NJ, 1959–64), 2 vols, i, chs.2–4.
15. Languedoc was the centre of French Protestantism, and the war of the Camisards, in which some Protestant rebels invoked William III as their potential saviour, lasted from 1702 to 1705. See Emmanuel Le Roy Ladurie, *Les Paysans de Languedoc* (Paris, 1966), 2 vols, ii, p.619.

16. Gerard O'Brien, *Anglo-Irish Politics in the Age of Grattan and Pitt* (Dublin, 1987), pp.31–32.

17. See Antoine, *Conseil du Roi* , pp.292–296, 515–518.

18. P.G.M. Dickson, *Finance and Government under Maria Theresia 1740–1780* (Oxford, 1987), 2 vols, i, chs.10–11, ii, pp.1–35.

19. T.W. Bartlett, 'The augmentation of the army in Ireland, 1767–1788' *English Historical Review*, xcvi (1981), pp.540–559.

20. Daniel Stone, *Polish Politics and National Reform, 1775–1788* (Boulder, CO, 1976); see also the papers collected in Samuel Fiszman (ed.) *Constitution and Reform in Eighteenth Century Poland* (Bloomington, IND, 1997).

21. Butterwick, *Poland's Last King*, ch.7.

22. Boguslaw Leśnodorski, *Les Jacobins polonais* (Paris, 1965).

23. The classic survey is in chs.3 and 4 of Simon Schama, *Patriots and Liberators. Revolution in the Netherlands, 1780–1813* (London, 1977).

24. Janet Polasky, *Revolution in Brussels 1787–1793* (Brussels, 1986).

25. Béla K. Király, *Hungary in the Later Eighteenth Century* (New York, 1969).

26. Echeverria, *Maupeou Revolution*, pp.37–122.

27. In the Ulster Museum there are buttons from Volunteer tunics with these words inscribed.

28. O'Brien, *Anglo-Irish Politics*, p.166.

29. Robert D. Harris, *Necker, Reform Statesman of the Ancien Regime* (Berkeley, Los Angeles and London, 1979), pp.176–191. See also M. Léonce de Lavergne, *Les Assemblées provinciales sous Louis XVI* (Paris, 1879), passim.

30. P. M. Jones, *Reform and Revolution in France. The Politics of Transition, 1774–1791* (Cambridge, 1995), pp.139–156.

31. Doyle, *Parlement of Bordeaux*, p.227.

32. Jones, *Reform and Revolution*, pp.37–38.

33. Jean-Pierre Jessenne, Gilles Deregnaucourt, Jean-Pierre Hirsch, Hervé Leuwers (eds.) *Robespierre. De la nation artésienne à la république et aux nations* (Lille, 1994), pp.73–104.

34. See the other papers presented originally at the same conference as this one: *Transactions of the Royal Historical Society*, sixth series, 10 (2000), pp.181–408.

35. Bolton, *Passing of the Irish Act of Union*, pp.6–7; O'Brien, *Anglo-Irish Politics*, p.50.

36. O'Brien, *Anglo-Irish Politics*, ch.6.

37. See Burdette C. Poland, *French Protestantism and the French Revolution. A study in Church and State, Thought and Religion, 1685–1815* (Princeton, NJ, 1957), passim.

38. Thomas W. Bartlett, *The Fall and Rise of the Irish Nation. The Catholic Question 1690–1830* (Dublin, 1992), chs.8 and 9; Dáire Keogh, *The 'French Disease'. The Catholic Church and Irish Radicalism, 1790–1800* (Dublin, 1997).

39. In Europe at least: the same strategy had of course underlain the Quebec Act of 1774, itself passed to reinforce the loyalty of Catholic French Canadians at a time when Protestant subjects of the king were on the verge of rebellion in the 13 colonies.

40. Bartlett, *Fall and Rise*, p.151.

41. T.C.W. Blanning, *The Origins of the French Revolutionary Wars* (London, 1986), p.211.

42. See Harling, *Waning of 'Old Corruption'*, pp.104–106, 261–262.

Chapter 6. The French Revolution: Possible because Thinkable or Thinkable because possible?

This chapter, now slightly amended, first appeared in *Proceedings of the Western Society for French History*, 30 (2004), pp.178–183. I am grateful to the editors of the series for permission to reproduce it. It was first presented at the annual meeting of the Society in Baltimore in 2002. I am also grateful to Daniel Gordon for orchestrating that session, to Keith Baker and David Bell for their comments during it, and to Barry Rothaus for publishing the paper in the *Proceedings*.

1. 'On the Problem of the Ideological Origins of the French Revolution' in *Inventing the French Revolution: Essays on French Political Culture in the Eighteenth Century* (Cambridge, 1990), pp.12–27.

2. 'Public Opinion as Political invention', in *Inventing the French Revolution*, pp.167–199.

3. *Les Origines culturelles de la Révolution française* (Paris, 1990), p.10. My translation.

4. *The Cult of the Nation in France. Inventing Nationalism 1680–1800* (Cambridge, MA, 2001), p.125.

5. 'The Great Enlightenment Massacre' in Haydn T. Mason (ed.) *The Darnton Debate. Books and Revolution in the Eighteenth Century* (Oxford, 1998), p.152.

6. 'Inventing the French Revolution' in *Inventing the French Revolution*, pp.203–223.

7. Baker, 'A script for the French Revolution: the Political Consciousness of the Abbé Mably' in *Inventing the French Revolution*, pp.86–106.

8. Doyle, *Origins of the French Revolution* (1st edn., 1980), p.213. The same conclusion is in both subsequent editions. Timothy Tackett, *Becoming a Revolutionary. The Deputies of the French National Assembly and the Emergence of a Revolutionary Culture (1789–1790)* (Princeton, NJ, 1996).

9. 'Fixing the French Constitution' in *Inventing the French Revolution*, p.305.

10. *French Historical Studies*, 16 (1990), p.759.

Chapter 7. Desacralising Desacralisation

This chapter is a translation of 'Une Désacralisation à désacraliser? *À propos d'une interprétation récente de la monarchie française au XVIIIᵉ siècle'* in Anne-Marie

Cocula and Josette Pontet (eds.) *Itinéraires spirituels, enjeux matériels en Europe. Mélanges offerts à Philippe Loupès*, ii, *Au contact des Lumières* (Bordeaux, 2005), pp.382–390. I am grateful to Presses Universitaires de Bordeaux for permission to reprint this slightly amended version.

1. Philippe Loupès, *La Vie religieuse en France au XVIIIᵉ siècle* (Paris, 1993), p.152.
2. Sarah E. Melzer and Kathryn Norberg (eds.) *From the Royal to the Republican Body. Incorporating the Political in seventeenth and eighteenth century France* (Berkeley, CA, 1998), p.7.
3. Van Kley, *The Jansenists and the Expulsion of the Jesuits.*
4. *The Damiens Affair and the Unraveling of the Ancien Regime, 1750–1770* (Princeton, NJ, 1984).
5. Ibid., p.255.
6. *The Desacralisation of the French Monarchy in the eighteenth century* (Baton Rouge, LA, 1990), p.167.
7. *The Religious Origins of the French Revolution. From Calvin to the Civil Constitution, 1560–1791* (New Haven, CT, 1996), p.164.
8. *The Forbidden Bestsellers of pre-revolutionary France* (London, 1996), p.236.
9. Ibid., p.237.
10. *Dire et mal dire. L'opinion publique au XVIIIᵉ siècle* (Paris, 1992).
11. *Les Origines culturelles de la Révolution française.*
12. Edmé Champion, *La France d'après les cahiers de 1789* (Paris, 1897), pp.236–237; Pierre Goubert and Michel Denis, *1789. Les Français ont la parole* (Paris, 1964), pp.39–49. See also Timothy Tackett, *When the King took Flight* (Cambridge, MA, 2003), pp.182–184.
13. Richard A. Jackson, *Vive le Roi! A History of the French Coronation from Charles V to Charles X* (Chapel Hill, NC, 1984); Ralph E. Giesey, *The Royal Funeral Ceremony in Renaissance France* (Geneva, 1960).
14. *Dire et mal dire*, p.202.
15. Thomas E. Kaiser, 'Louis le Bien- Aimé and the rhetoric of the Royal Body' in Melzer and Norberg, *From the Royal to the Republican Body*, pp.149–152.
16. Arlette Farge and Jacques Revel, *Logique de la foule. L'affaire de l'enlèvement des enfants, Paris, 1750* (Paris, 1988).
17. Simon Burrows, *Blackmail, Scandal, and Revolution. London's French* libellistes, *1758–92* (Manchester, 2006).
18. See the previous chapter in this collection.
19. *La Révolution. De Turgot à Jules Ferry 1770–1880* (Paris, 1988), pp.89–90; see also François Furet and Ran Halévi, *La Monarchie républicaine. La constitution de 1791* (Paris, 1996).
20. Loupès, *La vie religieuse en France*, pp.151–152.
21. The consensus of all who have studied this episode recently: John Hardman, *Louis XVI* (London, 1993); Munro Price, *The Fall of the French Monarchy. Louis XVI, Marie-Antoinette and the Baron de Breteuil* (London, 2002); Tackett, *When the King took Flight.*

Chapter 8. The French Revolution
and Monarchy

This chapter first appeared in Robert Smith and John S. Moore (eds.) *The Monarchy. Fifteen Hundred Years of British Tradition* (London, 1998). I am grateful to Robert Smith for permission to reprint it, and to him and John Moore for the invitation to present it at a meeting of the Manorial Society of Great Britain at Pembroke College, Oxford, in 1996.

1. Furet, *La Révolution, 1770–1880*; Simon Schama, *Citizens. A Chronicle of the French Revolution* (New York and London, 1989).
2. Hardman, *Louis XVI*.
3. See ch.7, above.
4. Hardman, *Louis XVI*, pp.121, 144.
5. Michael Roberts, 'The Dubious Hand: the history of a controversy' in *From Oxenstierna to Charles XII* (Cambridge, 1991), pp.144–203.
6. Hardman, *Louis XVI*, ch.14.
7. See David P. Jordan, *The King's Trial. Louis XVI versus the French Revolution* (Berkeley, Los Angeles and London, 1979), chs.ix-xi; and, more generally, Michael Walzer, *Regicide and Revolution. Speeches at the trial of Louis XVI* (Cambridge, 1974).
8. Lynn Hunt, *The Family Romance of the French Revolution* (Berkeley, CA, 1992) ch.4.
9. See Irene Collins, *Napoleon and his Parliaments, 1800–1815* (London, 1979).

Chapter 9. The American Revolution and the
European Nobility

This chapter has not been previously published.

1. Gordon S. Wood, *The Creation of the American Republic, 1776–1787* (Chapel Hill, NC, 1969); *The Radicalism of the American Revolution* (New York, 1991).
2. Merrill Jensen, *The Articles of Confederation* (Madison, WI, 1940), p.255.
3. *Discourses*, i, 55.
4. *Esprit des Lois*, ii, ch.4.
5. Wood, *Radicalism*, pp.182–183.
6. *Defence of the Constitutions of Government of the United States of America* (1788).
7. See Edmond Dziembowski, *Un Nouveau Patriotisme français, 1750–1770* (SVEC 365, Oxford, 1998); David A. Bell, *The Cult of the Nation in France,*

Inventing Nationalism, 1680–1800 (Cambridge, MA, 2001); Jay M. Smith, *Nobility Reimagined. The Patriotic Nation in Eighteenth Century France* (Ithaca, NY, 2005).

8. Louis Gottschalk, *Lafayette comes to America* (Chicago, IL 1935); *Lafayette joins the American Army* (Chicago, IL 1937); Lloyd Kramer, *Lafayette in Two Worlds. Public Cultures and Personal Identities in an Age of Revolutions* (Chapel Hill, NC, 1996), ch.1.

9. Adam Zamoyski, *Holy Madness. Romantics, Patriots and Revolutionaries 1776–1871* (London, 1999), pp.24–25.

10. Ibid., p.29; see also M.K. Dziewanowski, 'Tadeusz Kościuszko, Kazimierz Pułaski, and the War of American Independence: a study in national symbolism and mythology' in Jaroslaw Pelenski (ed.) *The American and European Revolutions, 1776–1848* (Iowa City, IA 1980), pp.125–146.

11. J.M. Palmer, *General von Steuben* (New Haven, CT, 1937).

12. Quoted in H. Arnold Barton, *Scandinavia in the Revolutionary Era, 1760–1800* (Minneapolis, MI, 1986), p.122. On Fersen in America, idem, *Count Hans Axel von Fersen. Aristocrat in an Age of Revolution* (Boston, MA, 1975), ch.2.

13. Estimated from Gilbert Bodinier, *Dictionnaire des Officiers de l'Armée royale qui ont combattu aux États-Unis pendant la Guerre d'Indépendance, 1776–1783* (Vincennes, 1983); Christian de Jonquière, *Officiers de Marine aux Cincinnati: Annuaire* (Toulouse, 1988); Zamoyski, *Holy Madness*, p.29; Barton, *Scandinavia*, p.114.

14. See William Doyle, *Aristocracy and its Enemies in the Age of Revolution* (Oxford, 2009), ch.4; Minor Myers, Jr., *Liberty without Anarchy. A history of the Society of the Cincinnati* (Charlottesville, VA, 1983); Markus Hünemörder, *The Society of the Cincinnati. Conspiracy and Distrust in Early America* (New York and Oxford, 2006).

15. Quoted in Doyle, *Aristocracy and its Enemies*, p.109.

16. Ibid., pp.109–110.

17. Ibid., p.120.

18. Quoted ibid., p.131.

19. Myers, *Liberty without Anarchy*, p.66.

20. Doyle, *Aristocracy and its Enemies*, pp.86–87.

21. Ibid., pp.113–116.

22. 26 January 1784, in J.A. Leo Le May (ed.) *Benjamin Franklin. Writings* (New York, 1987), pp.1084–1089.

23. *Considerations on the Order of Cincinnatus … translated from the French of the Count de Mirabeau* (London, 1785), p.62. On Mirabeau and America in general, see François Quastana, *La Pensée politique de Mirabeau (1771–1789). « Républicanisme classique » et régénération de la monarchie* (Aix-en-Provence, 2007), pp.366–375.

24. Palmer *Age of the Democratic Revolution*. i, p.244.

25. See Smith, *Nobility Reimagined*, ch.3; and John Shovlin, *The Political Economy of Virtue. Luxury, Patriotism and the Origins of the French Revolution* (Ithaca, NY, 2006), ch.2.

26. See Doyle, *Aristocracy and its Enemies*, chs.3, 5.

27. Ibid., 148–152.

28. *Journal de la Société de 1789*, vi, 10 July 1790, pp.19–42.
29. Doyle, *Aristocracy and its Enemies*, pp.3–5, 233–238.

Chapter 10. The Napoleonic Nobility Revisited

This hitherto unpublished chapter began as a paper presented at the Society for French Historical Studies annual conference in St. Louis, MO in 2009.

1. Barry E. O'Meara, *Napoleon in Exile; or, a Voice from St. Helena*, (London, 1822), 2 vols, i, p.164.
2. Natalie Petiteau, *Elites et mobilités: la noblesse d'Empire au XIXᵉ siècle (1808–1914)* (Paris, 1997), p.50.
3. Félix Ponteil, *Napoléon 1ᵉʳ et l'organisation autoritaire de la France* (Paris, 1956), p.126.
4. Petiteau, 48; Jean Tulard, *Napoléon et la noblesse d'Empire* (Paris 3rd ed., 2001), pp.150–151.
5. Tulard, p.97.
6. Ibid., pp.37–39.
7. Ibid., p.93. But even Tulard admits that this is a minimum. Geoffrey Ellis, *The Napoleonic Empire* (London, 2003), p.87, believes that omissions probably carry the total to nearer 3,600.
8. Michel Nassiet, *Parenté, noblesse et états dynastiques, XVᵉ-XVIᵉ siècles* (Paris, 2000), pp.20–22; idem, 'Les effectifs de la noblesse en France sous l'ancien régime' in Jarosław Dumanowski and Michel Figeac (eds.) *Noblesse française et noblesse polonaise. Mémoire, identité, culture. XVIᵉ-XXᵉ siècles* (Bordeaux, 2006), pp.19–43.
9. Petiteau, pp.43–45.
10. Comte de Las Cases, *Le Mémorial de Sainte-Hélène* (ed. G. Walter, Paris, 1956), 2 vols, i, p.895.
11. Quoted in Jean Tulard (ed.) *Dictionnaire Napoléon* (2nd edn., Paris, 1989), p.1244.
12. Petiteau, pp.253–259.

Chapter 11. Napoleon, Women, and the French Revolution

This chapter has not previously been published.

1. See Dorothy Carrington, *Napoleon and his Parents. On the Threshold of History* (London, 1988).
2. Letter of 15 May 1807, in J.M. Thompson (ed.) *Letters of Napoleon* (Oxford, 1934), p.195.

3. See Angelica Gooden, *Madame de Staël. The Dangerous Exile* (Oxford, 2008).
4. Letter cited above, n.2.
5. Ibid.
6. If he did not choose instead to have her imprisoned.
7. Yvonne Knibiehler in Tulard, *Dictionnaire Napoléon*, pp.728–729.
8. See Joan B. Landes, *Women and the Public sphere in the Age of the French Revolution* (Ithaca, NY, 1988); Sara E. Melzer and Leslie W. Rabine (eds.) *Rebel Daughters. Women and the French Revolution* (New York and Oxford, 1992); Madelyn Gutwirth, *The Twilight of the Goddesses. Women and Representation in the French Revolutionary Era* (New Brunswick, NJ, 1992); Jean-Clément Martin, *La Révolte brisée. Femmes dans la Révolution française et l'Empire* (Paris, 2008).
9. Dena Goodman, *The Republic of Letters. A cultural History of the French Enlightenment* (Ithaca, NY, 1994).
10. Olwen H. Hufton, *Women and the Limits of Citizenship in the French Revolution* (Toronto, 1992), ch.3.
11. Marie Cerati, *Le Club des Citoyennes républicaines révolutionnaires* (Paris, 1966); Landes, *Women and the Public Sphere*, pp.139–146; Hufton, *Women and the Limits*, pp.28–39; Darline Gay Levy and Harriet B. Applewhite, 'Women and militant citizenship in Revolutionary Paris', in Melzer and Rabine, *Rebel Daughters*, pp.79–101; Gutwirth, *Twilight*, ch.7; Dominique Godineau, *The Women of Paris and their French Revolution* (Berkeley and Los Angeles, 1998), chs.6 & 7.
12. See 'Thomas Paine and the Girondins' in *Officers, Nobles and Revolutionaries*, pp.211–217.
13. J.M. Thompson, *The French Revolution* (Oxford, 1943), p.274.

Chapter 12. The Political Culture of the French Empire

This chapter first appeared in Alan Forrest and Peter H. Wilson (eds.) *The Bee and the Eagle. Napoleonic France and the End of the Holy Roman Empire, 1806* (Basingstoke, 2009), pp.83–93. I am grateful to Alan Forrest and Peter Wilson for an invitation to present the original version at a conference at the German Historical Institute in London in 2006.

1. (Oxford, 1987–1994) edited by Keith Michael Baker (vols.1 and 4), Colin Lucas (vol.2) and François Furet (vol.3).
2. Keith Michael Baker (ed.) *The French Revolution and the Creation of Modern Political Culture. Volume 1. The Political Culture of the Old Regime*, p.xii.
3. See J. Christopher Herold, *The Mind of Napoleon. A selection from his written and spoken words* (New York, 1955), p.109.
4. There was not the same objection in Italy as in France to the kingly title, and it was by virtue of this that the Emperor increasingly used the term 'imperial and royal majesty'. Was this perhaps also a riposte to the Habsburg formula of *kaiserlich und königlich*?

5. See Thierry Lentz, 'Napoléon et Charlemagne' in Thierry Lentz (ed.) *Napoléon et l'Europe* (Paris, 2005), pp.11–30.

6. See Annie Jourdan, *Napoléon. Héros, imperator, mécène* (Paris, 1998), pp.177–184.

7. And in 1806 Napoleon formally adopted his stepson, Eugène de Beauharnais. That he had made him Viceroy of Italy the year before suggests that he was preferred as a successor to the two brothers named in the *Senatusconsultum* of 18 May 1804 constituting the Empire. A presumptive adoptive son was in any case placed ahead of them in the line of succession.

8. Laurence Chatel de Brancion (ed.) *Cambacérès. Mémoires inédits* (2 vols, Paris, 1999), i, pp.714–715.

9. See Louis Madelin, *Histoire du Consulat et de L'Empire, v, L'avènement de l'Empire* (Paris, 1939), pp.107–109; Michel Pastoureau, 'Héraldique' in Tulard, *Dictionnaire Napoléon*, p.870.

10. Lucien Bély, 'Napoléon juge de Louis XIV' in Lentz, *Napoléon et l'Europe*, pp.29–40.

11. See Doyle, *Venality*, pp.313–314.

12. He would, he told Bertrand on St. Helena shortly before his final illness, have liked to restore the parlements, but it was not possible. Venality was 'too far from the ideas of the age and from those of the Revolution', there were too few rich old families to staff them, and they had exercised police powers, whereas 'police belongs to the administration and not to the judiciary': Paul Fleuriot de Langle (ed.) *Journal du Général Bertrand, Grand Maréchal du Palais. Cahiers de Saint-Hélène. Janvier 1821–Mai 1821* (Paris, 1949), pp.50–51, 27 January 1821.

13. Alexis de Tocqueville, *L'Ancien Régime et la Révolution*, Bk. ii, ch.2.

14. Quoted in André Cabanis, 'Presse' in Tulard (ed.) *Dictionnaire Napoléon*, p.1398.

15. J. Christopher Herold, *Mistress to an Age. A Life of Mme de Staël* (London, 1958), pp.385–391. See also Simone Balayé, 'Madame de Staël et le gouvernement impérial en 1810, le dossier de la suppression de *De l'Allemagne*', *Cahiers Staëliennes*, xliv, (1974).

16. Thompson (ed.) *Letters of Napoleon*, pp.148–149, 5 June 1806; Gooden, *Mme de Staël*, pp.191–198.

17. Jacques-François de Menou, who had been president of the National Assembly at the session in which hereditary nobility was abolished (19 June 1790) proposed six days later that all existing orders of chivalry should be replaced by a single 'national order'. At this stage the proposal was rejected. *Archives Parlementaires*, xvi, 464, 25 June 1790.

18. See the following chapter. Authoritative on this entire subject is Jean Tulard, *Napoléon et la noblesse d'Empire*.

Chapter 13. Revolutionary Napoleon

This hitherto unpublished chapter originated as the Wellington Memorial Lecture presented at the University of Southampton in 2009.

1. Quoted in Elizabeth Longford, *Wellington. The Years of the Sword* (St. Albans, 1971 edn.), p.318.
2. Philip Henry Earl Stanhope, *Notes on Conversations with the Duke of Wellington* [1886], ed. Elizabeth Longford (London, 1998), p.60.
3. Ibid., p.76.
4. Las Cases, *Mémorial*, i, pp.470–471, 9–10 April 1815.
5. Maximilien Vox (ed.) *Correspondance de Napoléon. Six cent lettres de travail (1806–1810)* (Paris, 1943), p.215. 12 April 1808.
6. Thompson, *Letters of Napoleon*, pp.44–46. 19 September, 1797.
7. Las Cases, *Mémorial*, i, p.268. 17 December 1815.
8. Malcolm Crook, 'Confidence from below? Collaboration and resistance in the Napoleonic plebiscites' in Michael Rowe (ed.) *Collaboration and resistance in Napoleonic Europe. State Formation in an Age of Upheaval, c.1800–1815* (Basingstoke, 2003), pp.19–36.
9. See above, ch.12.
10. Las Cases, *Mémorial*, ii, p.372, 18–19 July 1816.
11. See above, ch.11.
12. Michael Broers, *Europe under Napoleon, 1799–1815* (London, 1996).
13. See François Lebrun and Roger Dupuy (eds.) *Les Résistances à la Révolution* (Paris, 1987); D.M.G. Sutherland, *The French Revolution and Empire. The Quest for a Civic Order* (Oxford, 2003).
14. Stanhope, *Conversations*, as cited above, n.2.
15. See Jeremy Popkin, *You Are All Free. The Haitian Revolution and the Abolition of Slavery* (Cambridge, 2010).
16. Jeremy Adelman, *Sovereignty and Revolution in the Iberian Atlantic* (Princeton, 2006).

Index